IMAGES
of America

THEATRES OF THE SAN FRANCISCO PENINSULA

The *San Francisco Chronicle* "Peninsula Movie Guide" from June 23, 1957, with its sunshine icon at the top of the page, offers a nostalgic overview of the kind of fare that was being offered to moviegoers 50 years ago. From *Gunfight at the O.K. Corral* at the Seavue, Fox, and Manor, to *Lady Chatterley's Lover* at the Guild in Menlo Park, unquestionably there was something for everyone.

ON THE COVER: The 1950 gala reopening of Redwood City's Sequoia Theatre, now renamed Fox, was the stimulus for a citywide celebration. Fresh paint, new neon colors, and a completely redecorated interior ushered in the theater's third decade of operation. After 60 years, the Fox still stands as a downtown destination for entertainment-seeking visitors (pages 73–79).

IMAGES
of America

THEATRES OF THE SAN FRANCISCO PENINSULA

Jack Tillmany and Gary Lee Parks

ARCADIA
PUBLISHING

A lone memento of South San Francisco's Starlite Drive-In survives near its former location as a nostalgic reminder of an era now long gone but still alive in the memories of its patrons. (Gary Lee Parks.)

CONTENTS

ACKNOWLEDGMENTS

The authors wish to thank the following individuals and organizations who contributed materials and knowledge to this volume: Brisbane Library Historical Collection, Marta Cisneros, Colma Auto Body Shop (former Crest Theatre in Daly City), Colma Historical Association, the estate of Emma Ver-Linden, Half Moon Bay Historical Society, Mountain View Public Library, Los Altos History Museum, and Redwood City Public Library History Room.

We would also like to thank Robert Dickson, whose help and cooperation enabled us to access the B'Hend-Kaufmann Collection at the Margaret Herrick Library of the Academy of Motion Picture Arts and Sciences (photographs from this source are labeled AMPAS in the captions); Tom Gray, whose indefatigable determination to photograph every theater he could find 30 years ago has now provided us with the only known images of many of the sites, now long gone; Don Holmgren for his mapmaking skills and making visual sense of a burgeoning peninsula; David Keil for tirelessly researching theater opening and closing dates, seating capacities, and name changes; Barbara Kinchen, Mountain View city historian; Adam Martin of CinemaTour for the collection of drive-in photographs from the Syufy collection; Rebecca June Parks for additional proofreading and technical support; John Poultney, our editor, for his enthusiastic guidance and understanding; Martin Schmidt for the patiently shot contemporary neon night photographs; Richard Sklenar and Kathy McLeister; Theatre Historical Society of America for assistance in accessing the largest collection of theater building photographs in the United States; Edward Millington Stout III for providing the specifications of long-vanished theater pipe organs; Greg Timm, our guide in Pescadero; Terry Wade for the Serra Theatre demolition photograph; and Ed Weeks, former operator and projectionist of the Pescadero Theatre.

All photographs are from the Jack Tillmany collection unless otherwise identified.

INTRODUCTION

Having already guided our readers through *Theatres of San Francisco* and *Theatres of San Jose* in previously published volumes, we now set out to document the many places of amusement, past and present, located along the 50-mile stretch of turf that connects the two cities, locally known as "the Peninsula," or more casually, "the Bedroom of San Francisco." In more recent years, the moniker "Silicon Valley" has become widespread in describing the southern portion of the Peninsula north to Foster City, but that is a different ball game that we leave to other enterprising authors. During most of the time span with which we are dealing, Silicon Valley had not yet become part of the American vocabulary, so for the purposes of this book, the entire area will be referred to as the Peninsula.

During the first half of the 20th century, each of the communities was a self-contained entity, many of whose residents commuted daily to work in San Francisco, either by Southern Pacific train, Market Street Railway trolley, Greyhound bus, or automobile, but who lived their lives quite comfortably and happily in the more relaxed, less hectic environment of small-town America. In more recent years, most of the central Peninsula has grown to the point that each city is back to back with its next door neighbor, making it difficult to tell where one ends and the other begins. But to the people who live there, they all retain their individual identities, just as before.

A schematic map on the following page provides a bird's-eye view of the area in question for easy reference.

Happily, at least two of the most important vintage theaters in our survey are still in operation in the 21st century: the Fox (former Sequoia) in Redwood City, now home to live entertainment, and the Stanford in Palo Alto, restored to its 1920s grandeur by David W. Packard and for over 20 years since, a popular revival film and repertory venue. Several other sites have been converted to other uses, so they at least survive in one way or another, but most of them are gone forever. All of the many drive-ins, which were so much a part of their era, have disappeared completely, leaving rarely a trace. But they live in the memories of the countless throngs who once spent happy hours parked under the stars, dreaming of the wonderful future.

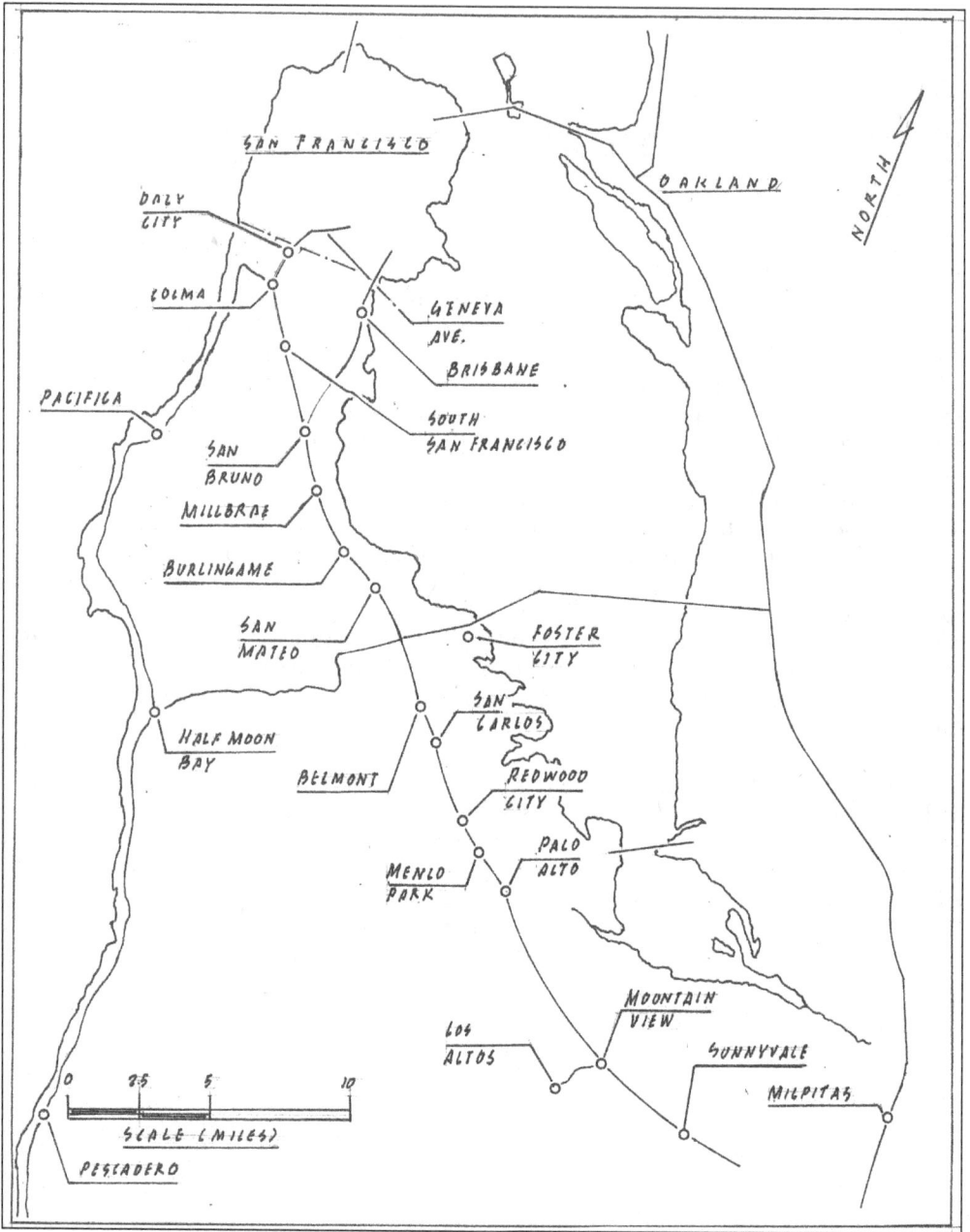

Prepared especially for this book, the map shows the locations of the cities and towns mentioned in the text and documented in photographs. Most communities are connected by the north-south routes of transportation—both highway and rail—that connect San Jose and San Francisco. Some cities, such as Palo Alto and most notably Redwood City (in its youth a shipping hub for the redwood timber industry), had harbors located on San Francisco Bay. The town of Half Moon Bay gave similar access directly to the Pacific Ocean.

One

THE NORTHERN
PENINSULA

The San Francisco Peninsula begins of course with San Francisco and continues southward with Daly City, which adjoins the city and county of San Francisco at its southern boundary, followed by Colma, South San Francisco, and San Bruno. To the west lies Pacifica, facing the Pacific Ocean, and to the east is Brisbane, overlooking San Francisco Bay. During the golden age of moviegoing, each community provided its residents with at least one theater, usually the anchor of the downtown business district and often within walking distance of the majority of its residents.

The Daly City, at 6212 Mission Street, was an example of what has long been described as an atmospheric theater, a style involving a smooth, vaulted plaster ceiling painted and lit to simulate a sky. Popularized by architects of the 1920s, lighting effects were provided to give the feeling of daylight, sunset, twilight, and night. A practical appeal to builders was that the ceiling did not need costly ornamentation.

The architectural styles employed in atmospheric theaters varied, but the effect was generally that of being under the sky in a courtyard, palace, or village setting. The Daly City included hints of Italianate style with a bit of Gothic and Spanish as well. In the pit is the shrouded console of the two-manual, six-rank Robert Morton pipe organ, the trusty voice of the silent screen, still in place in this 1942 photograph.

The Daly City opened November 27, 1928, and for over 20 years was Daly City's unrivalled motion picture venue. The theater had 1,250 seats, which were usually filled, both because of the intense popularity of moviegoing in general and because the Daly City was the only game in town. But then came drive-ins and television—and suddenly it was all over.

A last-minute marquee modernization in mid-1951 proved to be too little too late, and on December 22, 1955, the Daly City closed its doors for the last time, an early victim of the fast changing times, the emergence of television, and the Mission Drive-In, the trendy new kid on the block. After standing vacant for two years, the Daly City was torn down in February 1958 and a supermarket erected in its place.

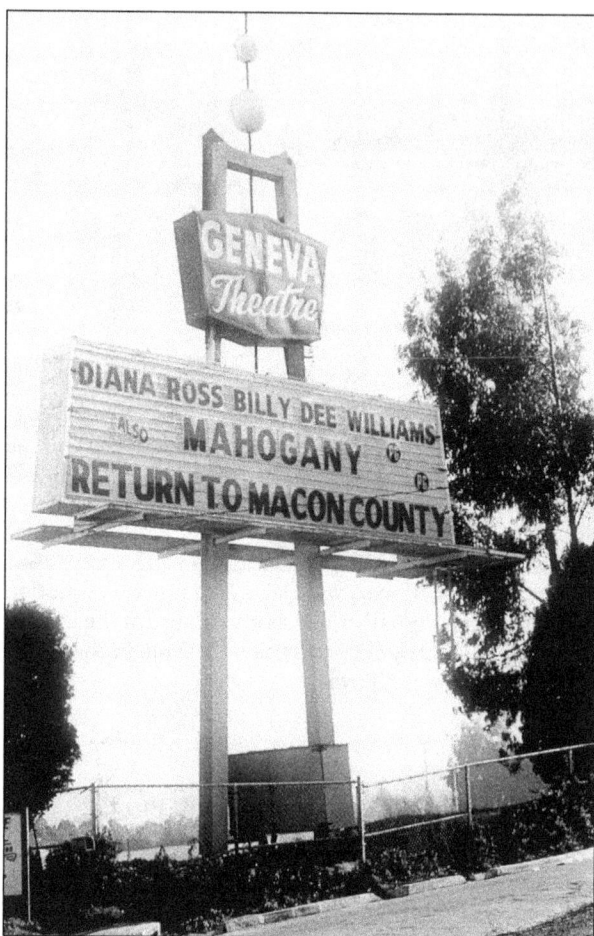

Built on the site of a midget auto racing track, the Geneva Drive-In, at 2150 Geneva Avenue, was always considered to be a San Francisco site but was actually located on the so-called other side of the county line in Daly City. A unique feature was an interior grandstand left over from its days as a racetrack; tucked underneath were a projection booth, refreshment stand, and restrooms.

Spread over 10 acres with the screen over 500 feet from the projection booth, there was no question that the Geneva covered plenty of ground. Two more screens were added in the 1970s, and its popularity continued well into the 1990s, but changing tastes and times ended its days in September 1998 after nearly a half century of popularity.

The official address of the Mission Drive-In, which opened on May 2, 1951, was 5500 Mission Street, San Francisco, but that was only its mailing address so that it could have a San Francisco identity. Like the Geneva, the actual site was situated across the county line atop Guttenberg Street in Daly City.

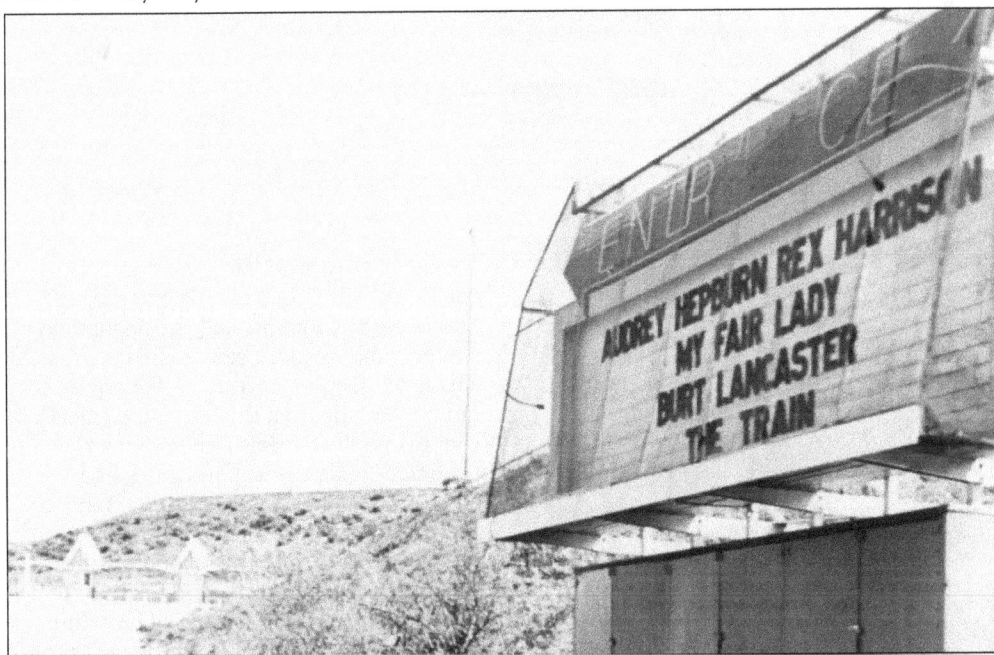

Although it was an immediate success from the very beginning (so much that its indoor neighbor the Daly City soon went out of business), the Mission eventually earned a reputation for harboring a pretty nasty clientele of local troublemakers, and the rest of its clientele eventually drifted to the nearby Geneva. Few tears were shed when it closed on October 5, 1976.

One of the first documented motion picture venues in Daly City was the Grand View at 6356 Mission Street on the northwest corner of Los Olivos Avenue. Daly City was known as "the Gateway to the Peninsula" at that time. It was the terminus for two major San Francisco trolley lines, Nos. 14 (Mission) and 26 (San Jose Avenue), both seen in this photograph, and from Daly City line No. 40 provided service all the way to San Mateo until 1949.

It must have seemed like a good idea at the time. Daly City had only one theater, business was booming, and the population was growing. So the Crest opened at 7252 Mission Street on April 2, 1948, doomed for failure. Judging from this surviving calendar, the first problem seems to be that by the time films reached the Crest, they had already been on the market for too long. In April 1950, the newest films offered were all 1949 releases, and the second features were often low budget B's and C's like *Arctic Fury* and *Trail of the Mounties*. The opening of the Serra in May 1950 and the nearby Mission and Geneva Drive-Ins soon triggered nature's oldest law, survival of the fittest, and the Crest closed its doors on September 23, 1951. (Colma Historical Museum.)

14

The Century 20, located at 1901 Junipero Serra Boulevard in Daly City, opened on June 21, 2002, and was an immediate success. It has proven to be a popular destination of choice for both Daly City and Colma residents, as well as its neighbors to the north in southwest San Francisco. Setting the standard for 21st-century moviegoing, similar sites would soon open in other communities and are visited later in the book. (Gary Lee Parks.)

Once located at 7379 Mission Street, the Colma Theatre (later renamed the New Colma) is virtually forgotten today, but this tiny snapshot survives to document its existence. Opening in the 1920s, its life extended into the sound era, but it soon succumbed to competition from the nearby Daly City (pages 10–11) and the financial woes of the Great Depression. (Colma Historical Association, the estate of Emma Ver-Linden.)

Despite its aborted existence as a movie theater, the Colma building has survived the last 80 years under various identities and today remains alive and well as the Globe Tavern. Almost immediately after its closure as a theater, the building was given a completely new Art Deco facade, which can be seen on the right in this 2010 photograph. (Gary Lee Parks.)

The Serra, at 2710 Junipero Serra Boulevard in Daly City, opened on May 18, 1950; it was one of the first postwar theaters to be built in this area. Designed in the familiar Moderne style, not unlike the somewhat larger Coronet in San Francisco that had opened six months earlier, it was sleek, modern, and functional with 1,000 seats arranged in the conventional stadium style.

For all the usual reasons, time took its toll on the Serra. Despite the highly successful 1975 long-run blockbuster *Jaws*, television and too much competition from newer nearby sites, both indoor and outdoor, caused business to deteriorate, and the division of Junipero Serra Boulevard to accommodate the 280 Freeway did not help. After standing vacant for several years, the Serra was finally torn down in 1998. (©Terryphoto.)

American Multi-Cinema's Serramonte 6, located at 4915 Junipero Serra Boulevard in Colma, opened on March 22, 1972, as Junipero Serra 6 with a total seating capacity of 1,700. It was renamed the Serramonte 6 the following December. The new name was not only easier to pronounce, it also helped identify its location near the Serramonte Shopping Center. Promoted as the first six-plex in the San Francisco Bay Area, it survived until December 1996, at which time it quietly closed and was soon torn down.

ABC Theatres' Plaza I & II, which opened at 311 Serramonte Plaza in Daly City on December 25, 1971, was built as a twin operation with two spacious auditoriums, each very much like the Northpoint, ABC's sister theater in San Francisco that had opened four years earlier. After a 25-year run, the Plaza I & II's audience had dwindled, its overhead had gone through the ceiling, and its doors closed for the last time in December 1996, the same month that Serramonte also closed.

Ill conceived and short lived, this was a unit of the Jerry Lewis circuit, a shoebox operation whose manager apparently could not even spell the name of the movie correctly. It opened on January 21, 1972, as Jerry Lewis Cinema, was renamed Westborough Square on June 7, 1972, and permanently closed December 5, 1972. Jerry Lewis's association with these cinemas, apart from lending them his name and trademark image, is unclear.

UA the Movies (later known as Metro Center 6) was located at 200 Colma Boulevard, opened in 1987, closed in 2003, and was torn down the following year. It was a transitional product of its era presented with as little imagination as its name and location implied—six screens in a big box with the four larger auditoriums seating 450 each and the two smaller ones seating 230.

Brisbane is a small (population 3,500), self-contained community on the eastern slopes of San Bruno Mountain overlooking San Francisco Bay. Geographically remote from its nearest neighbor, South San Francisco, its populace happily supported the 330-seat Brisbane Theatre, at 48 Visitacion Avenue, from the time it opened in 1941 well into the 1950s when easy freeway access to the Geneva Drive-In to the north and the inroads of television brought about its demise. (Brisbane Library History Collection.)

Getting a job at a local movie theater was once the dream of many high school graduates in small towns like Brisbane. Perhaps it was the first step in a business career that would eventually lead to San Francisco, perhaps an easy and socially acceptable way of meeting a life partner, or maybe—for the lucky—both. These two 1954 hopefuls are Vicki Trantham (left) and Juanita Blanchard. (Brisbane Library History Collection.)

South San Francisco's first theater, the Royal, operated on Grand Avenue from 1912 to 1918; the name derived from its operators, brothers Roy and Al Eiselback. In this 1916 photograph, the question that is obviously going through the minds of these potential filmgoers is whether *Wild Oats* is worth the 20¢ investment. In 1918, the first Royal was replaced by a second one at 211 Linden Street, which operated until 1931 when it was superseded by the state-of-the-art State.

The State, promoted by the Bayshore Theatre Corporation as the "Pride of the Peninsula" and located at 201 Linden Street in South San Francisco, opened on October 2, 1931, with 1,064 seats. Architects James and Merritt Reid, of San Francisco, had long been established as the most prolific designers of theaters in Northern California. Advertised in the lobby, Keno was a bingo-like screen game that attracted families during midweek when business was slowest in the 1930s; the game was still popular in the 1940s.

In the State auditorium, an atmospheric design, patrons were surrounded by false building facades complete with artificial trees and vines, while above a smooth plaster ceiling was painted and lit to simulate a sky. Tiny lightbulbs set into the plaster surface evoked twinkling stars. While the Daly City (pages 10–11) was also an atmospheric theater, the State carried off the effect with a bit more realism.

Theater signage was altered to reflect changing styles. By the late 1930s, a streamlined vertical sign had already been installed above the original marquee, as seen in this 1942 photograph. A Moderne support structure linked the sign to the original Spanish facade. After a successful reign of over 40 years, the State shut its doors as a movie theater on March 13, 1973, but its days were far from over, as seen below.

The building now houses an establishment called the State Room. Its atmospheric auditorium, somewhat modified structurally, hosts private events such as weddings, banquets, and meetings. The outer lobby functions as retail space. In this 2010 photograph, the State has been stripped of its later additions, revealing the original ornamentation that greeted the public in 1931—and Shell has supplanted 76 as the brand of gasoline sold on the adjacent corner. (Gary Lee Parks.)

The Starlite Drive-In, located at 30 South Linden Avenue in South San Francisco (see also page 4), opened on August 19, 1948, about a year after its sister theater (also named the Starlite) opened at 150 Harbor Boulevard in Belmont. During the postwar drive-in boom, there were between 150 and 200 sites operating around the country, all under the magic name of Starlite. Today, only a handful of Starlites remain in operation. (AMPAS.)

Long before flea markets became the rage, drive-ins took up valuable acreage that remained idle during daytime hours. So it was inevitable that—as with other endangered species now on the verge of extinction due to loss of habitat—they too would disappear, victims of changing times and ever-increasing land values. The Starlite would get a stay of execution in the mid-1960s when it was redeveloped into the Spruce Drive-In (page 28), but like the rest, it eventually succumbed to the relentless march of progress. (AMPAS.)

The cover of the Starlite's bimonthly calendar gives a couple of clues as to what it was about drive-ins that made them so popular: "Come as you are, fill up your car." The days of dressing up to go to the movies had passed; moviegoers wore whatever was comfortable, and the admission price was often by the carload, so the children in the back seat could wear their pajamas and were not charged separate admission.

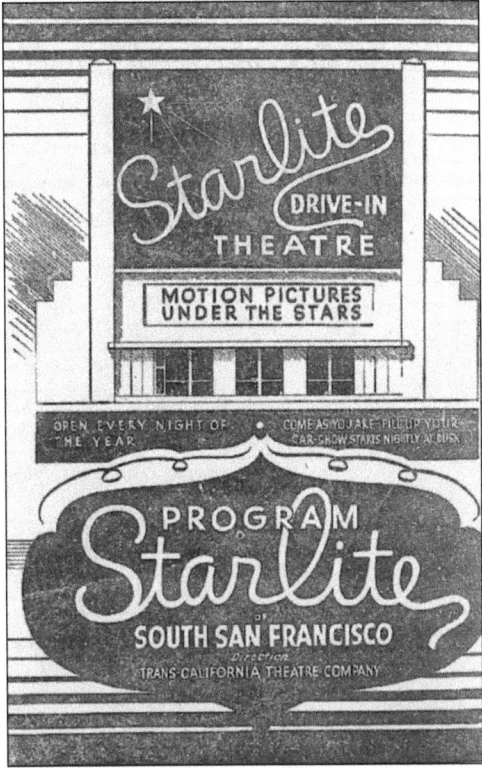

The frequency of movie attendance in the pre-television era is hard to imagine today. This two-month Starlite calendar offers three separate double-feature programs per week, an inviting mixture of the best of Hollywood's contemporary output with a generous number of past successes from previous years.

In the tradition of the West...

. . . Everything about El Rancho is *big* . . . Proportions are tremendous and the difficulties of construction were in the same staggering ratio . . . The ten acre amphitheatre was literally carved from a hill in a monumental leveling operation.

. . . Its great steel towers, supporting one of the world's largest screens . . . its parking ramps, readily accessible to modern elongated cars . . . were painstakingly engineered so that vision from either front or back seat of your car is unimpaired . . . and the picture undistorted from any angle . . .

. . . To project the huge images, yet maintain brilliant clarity, mammoth equipment was especially manufactured . . . and which can be inspected from windows located in El Rancho's immaculate snack bar . . .

. . . Sound impulses travel over a veritable web of underground wiring . . . to be reproduced into each car with amazing fidelity by individually volume-controlled speakers . . .

. . . In short, we feel that, out of a welter of detail and planning, no consideration has been overlooked for your complete comfort and convenience . . . And we trust all must recognize that our natural pride in an undertaking of such gallant proportions demands entertainment of no lesser magnitude through the weeks to come.

No comment can compare with the florid prose of the opening announcement of El Rancho Drive-In. Readers are advised to take a deep breath and read this document from top to bottom, word for word. Quipping that this flyer "says it all" would be quite the understatement.

El Rancho Drive-In at 517 Hickey Boulevard, near El Camino Real, opened on May 26, 1949, taking advantage of the undeveloped acres of inexpensive land between Colma and South San Francisco, which remained virtually untouched in this 1969 photograph. Note that side wings have now been added to the original narrower screen to properly project wide-screen films. Sound was broadcast over FM radio for better quality, thus eliminating the need for individual car speakers.

By 1975, El Rancho had added a second screen, theoretically to increase business by offering a wider range of product, but unfortunately often only affording an opportunity to air films better left in the can, as is the case with the now-forgotten foursome listed on the marquee in the photograph. By the 1980s, declining revenue and too many foggy nights ended it all, and the land was put to better and more profitable use with the construction of condominium apartments.

The Spruce Drive-In at 55 Spruce Avenue in South San Francisco opened on May 10, 1966, in direct competition with the by-then-elderly El Rancho less than five miles away. In the 1970s, three more screens were added, and the playground was a popular attraction to keep children amused during intermissions. By the 1980s, the land had become too valuable to waste on such frivolities; it closed and was demolished in favor a more financially practical industrial park.

A wall prevents drivers from sneaking from one parking area to another, but it is no impediment to them peeking over the top to see what's happening on the screen next door; children bored with watching Mary Poppins could always check out The Texas Chainsaw Massacre on the screen to the left or vice versa.

Prior to incorporation, the geographical center of today's community of Pacifica was called Pacific Manor. In May 1951, longtime San Francisco exhibitor Samuel C. Levin opened the first theater in the area, a $100,000 venue named the Seavue for its location just 300 feet from the thundering waves of the Pacific. A tower of green corrugated plastic housed a revolving array of neon tubes, giving a lighthouse effect to this fogbound community's singular movie house. (AMPAS.)

The lobby of the Seavue softly combined elements of Moderne, which was on its way out, and Mid-Century Modern, which was on its way in. A boxy lighting soffit heralded the new style, and wall decorations of nautical scenes combined with a bird-of-paradise pattern on the carpet harkened back to a look born in the 1930s. (AMPAS.)

Following World War II, architects no longer considered exposed wooden structural elements to be reserved only for rustic cabins and ski lodges. Ceilings of varnished, laminated wood beams and tongue-in-groove paneling became quite popular for theaters, churches, markets, and homes. Murals continued to be a feature of theaters, and the Seavue's glowed in the light of ultraviolet bulbs. Gale Santocono was the artist. (AMPAS.)

As with many single-level theaters of the era, a higher-priced loge section with comfortable seats was located at the rear. The seaside climate made air-conditioning unnecessary. In the mid-1950s came the demand for wide-screen projection, and the Seavue simply took down its excess draperies to reveal a proscenium happily quite wide enough for CinemaScope presentations. (AMPAS.)

Widening of the street out front required removal of the Seavue's porte cochere and the sign above. A new tower featuring boomerang shapes characteristic of the impending Space Age was installed over the entrance, a unique signature easily visible from the highway. In later years, competition from nearby multiplexes in Daly City and Colma lured the Seavue's already limited audience base to more up-to-date pastures, and an unfortunate twinning failed to compensate for the loss of revenue. It closed in 2002 and was torn down in 2008.

What are a folding chair, table, and typewriter doing in a theater lobby? The sign in the background says it all: "Buy War Bonds for VICTORY!" All theaters, large and small, contributed their share of war bond sales during the 1940s for the war effort. During the war, some theaters started the show with an image of Old Glory waving against the sky, complete with a recorded soundtrack of the national anthem. Here, San Bruno's El Camino Theatre is seen doing its part.

By the time El Camino was captured in this wartime-era photograph, the Wurlitzer Style D Special organ had been removed. So, along with various other cosmetic touches as part of a later redecoration, the angled organ chambers on either side of the stage and screen were plastered-over and given murals in a blend of Art Deco and Baroque that is sometimes called the Hollywood Regency style. Stadium seating, today a recent design feature, actually was quite common in midsize theaters from the 1920s through the 1940s, as evidenced here.

El Camino opened on July 29, 1930, at 408 San Mateo Avenue in San Bruno, the first—and for the next 40 years—only major indoor house in that area. The presence of El Camino Creamery next door is typical of its era when so-called creameries (sandwich shops) adjoining theaters often overflowed thanks to the never-ending (they thought) crowds of moviegoers before and after the show.

By the 1970s, a poorly maintained and aging structure was no competition for the multitude of more modern indoor sites and drive-ins popping up elsewhere, and El Camino closed its doors for the last time on August 16, 1973. In later years, the revamped building found new life as El Camino Plaza with now defunct Eureka Federal Savings as its anchor, but it currently stands vacant and abandoned. (Gary Lee Parks.)

Opening with much fanfare on June 29, 1966, the Fox Skyline was one of the last single-screen enterprises to be built from the ground up and was the intended anchor of the Skyline Plaza shopping center at Skyline Boulevard and Sharp Park Road in the hills of San Bruno. But it was an ill-fated venture. Within a few years, multiplexes would provide more economical motion picture exhibition, and the Fox Skyline would soon be history. (AMPAS.)

The Fox Skyline suffered from two insurmountable problems. Its local audience base was too few in number to provide the necessary financial support for a single-screen theater, and its fog-shrouded location was virtually impenetrable to members of the outside world on many a misty night. Business deteriorated in the 1970s, and its doors closed on March 22, 1978. In the mid-1980s, the entire shopping center was demolished and an apartment complex built on the site.

At the time of the Fox Skyline's demolition, its style was already passé. Today, collectors of 1960s fixtures would have an architectural salvage field day. The curve of the coved ceiling is a lobby feature with its roots in the 1930s and 1940s, but otherwise, the Fox Skyline welcomed its public with elegantly simple Futurism. The box office was contained in the lobby. By the 1960s, freestanding box offices of old had proven vulnerable to thieves and vandals, and many were removed, while newer theaters eschewed them altogether. (AMPAS.)

The Fox Skyline's auditorium shows the typical minimalist design of the 1960s—as little design possible with no decoration. The wide screen—the most significant change in movie exhibition since World War II—was the center of it all, but there was still something grand amidst the austerity. The raked seating, the graceful arc of the ceiling slot where the curtains parted and closed, and the saucer-shaped air registers in the ceiling managed to suggest that this was a room where fantasy reigned. (AMPAS.)

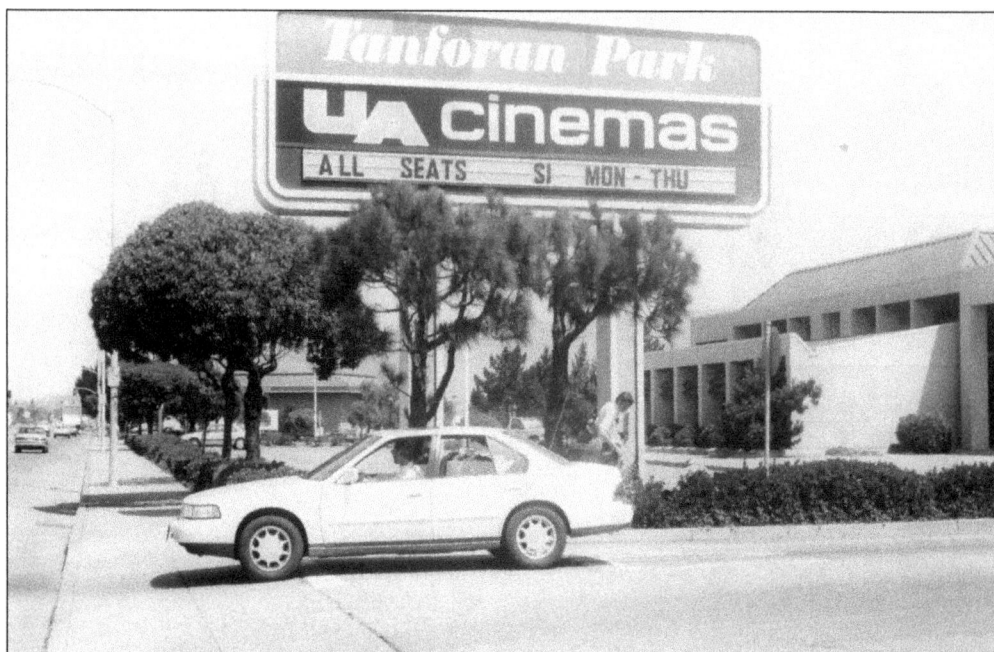

UA Cinemas 4 was an uninviting four-plex shoebox theater that opened at the Tanforan Park Shopping Center on December 19, 1974, and a failure from the beginning. Even lowering the admission price to a dollar on Monday through Thursday evenings failed to attract an audience. It mercifully disappeared and has since been superseded by the gargantuan Century 14 at Tanforan.

Consisting of two domes and six shoeboxes, Century 8 opened on June 3, 1985, at 410 Noor Avenue in South San Francisco. The domes were later split in half, and it was renamed Century Plaza 10. By 2008, it was declared obsolete and shut down, as Century offered moviegoers a more contemporary 21st-century moviegoing experience at the nearby Century 14 at Tanforan.

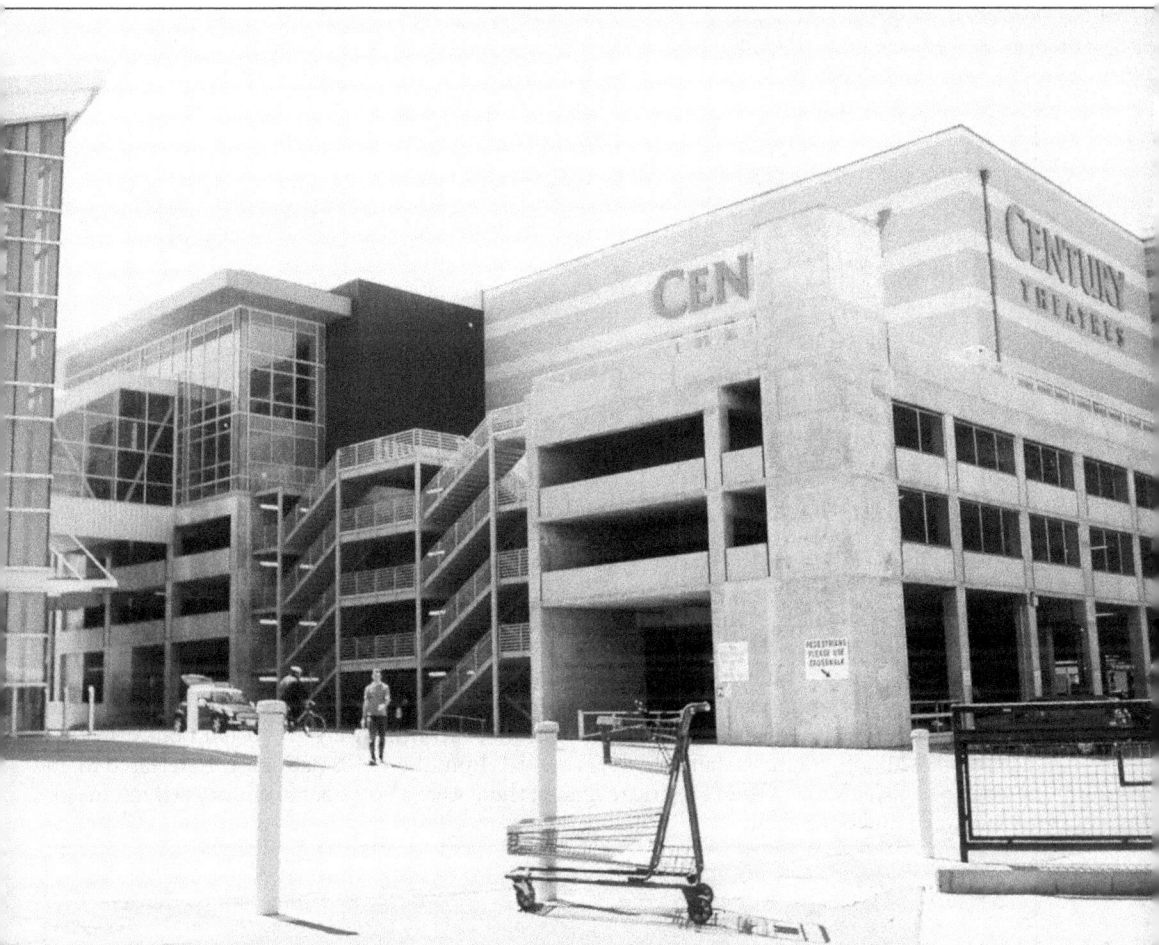

Movie theaters of the early 21st century can boast of square footage and seating capacities comparable to the largest movie palaces of decades ago. The difference is that spatial volume and seat numbers are spread over multiple auditoria. The Century 14 at Tanforan is, for the most part, typical of many theaters of the present day. Emphasis is on technology over architectural fantasy, although some modern multiscreen theaters make a more valiant effort at creating ambience, as will be seen later. (Gary Lee Parks.)

The Millbrae opened on July 14, 1949, at 49 El Camino Real in Millbrae. With 1,052 comfortable seats and plenty of room for wide-screen projection when it arrived in the 1950s, it was, quite simply, a great place to see a movie. Although first-run films were the usual policy, in this October 1972 photograph, its marquee offers revivals from the 1940s nationally re-released in an attempt to bolster MGM's then sagging revenues; there were also a couple of tasty attractions for a Halloween midnight show.

Converted to a tri-plex in 1980, the Millbrae closed in 1995. The storefront and lobby portions of the building were demolished for a parking lot, and the auditorium block was converted to retail. The City of Millbrae required the developer to retain the striking vertical neon sign, which was relocated to a new spot in the center of the former auditorium structure, which first housed Hollywood Video and more recently a bank. (Fred Beall, Theatre Historical Society.)

Two

MID-PENINSULA— SOUTHERN SAN MATEO COUNTY

Drawing an imaginary line between Millbrae and Burlingame continues the journey southward to what will be referred to as Mid-Peninsula, comprising the theaters located in the various communities of southern San Mateo County. In geographical order, Burlingame, San Mateo, and Redwood City boast the largest populations and, appropriately, the most ornate and impressive theaters of the lot, including the Peninsula, the San Mateo, and the Sequoia, all built in the 1920s. San Carlos residents enjoyed the more modern Carlos and Laurel Theatres, built respectively just before and just after World War II. Belmont and Menlo Park are also represented, as well as Half Moon Bay and Pescadero on the coast. Drive-in attendance peaked in the late 1940s and early 1950s, and the authors are happy to provide documentation in words and photographs of many popular peninsula drive-in theaters, all of them now gone. Two large live venues, the Hyatt Music Theatre in Burlingame and the Circle Star Theatre in San Carlos, enjoyed their moment, commanding huge audiences during the golden days of live theater-in-the-round performances.

The Peninsula Theatre at 1415 Burlingame Avenue in Burlingame opened on October 12, 1926. With a seating capacity of 1,808, it was the second of three movie palaces (regal in every sense of the word) built in mid–San Mateo County during the moviegoing peak of the last half of the 1920s. The San Mateo (pages 52–54) was the first, and the Sequoia in Redwood City (pages 73–79) was the third. In this 1933 photograph, the Peninsula shows its original multi-toned paint job and double-sided rooftop sign, which animated the theater's name in lightbulbs, a popular promotional conceit of the 1920s.

The original marquee of the Peninsula was outlined in twinkling bulbs and backlit stained-glass panels. Patrons expected extravagantly decorated fronts to herald important attractions, but in 1939 the Peninsula went one better. A papier-mâché Tyrone Power straddling the box office as Jesse James was not that unusual, but the opportunity to purchase tickets through the open crotch of his buckskin britches took showmanship to the limit.

Working from a San Francisco office, Charles Peter Weeks and William Day were the Peninsula Theatre's architects. San Francisco's Mark Hopkins and Sir Francis Drake Hotels were also products of their ingenuity, and they had already designed Palo Alto's Stanford Theatre (pages 97–103). Within months, their California Theatre in San Jose would debut as well. Weeks and Day were masters at grand staircases and towering lobbies, and the Peninsula had both.

The larger theaters balanced their grand lobbies and cavernous auditoriums with intimate spaces, providing an added sense of luxury. In the mezzanine lounge shown, sofas, throne chairs, and even a padded bench in front of the baronial fireplace invite patrons to linger before or after the show. Framed oil paintings, wrought-iron light fixtures with parchment shades, and a wall-mounted cluster of faux weaponry further enhance the atmosphere.

Here is the Peninsula's auditorium viewed from the balcony. Chandeliers of wrought iron and stenciled mica illuminate a room with Spanish and Italian design elements. The graceful sweep of the coffered ceiling provides grandeur and good acoustics. The voices of the three-manual, 13-rank Robert Morton organ spoke through the twin arched grilles, flanked by Corinthian columns. The asbestos fire curtain—painted with a Spanish galleon—could be lowered in case of a backstage fire.

By 1956, after 30 successful years of operation, the Peninsula remained remarkably unchanged, planted like a fortress anchoring the Burlingame Avenue downtown business district. The facade had doubtlessly been repainted several times in whatever was the color palette of the moment in any given decade. The marquee, too, must have been spruced up even more often, and a contemporary 1950s backlit reader board announced the current attraction. But the Peninsula's age was showing. (AMPAS.)

By the mid-1950s, snack bars had become a major source of revenue and profit, saving—or at least extending—the lives of many movie theaters facing financial difficulties. In typical Fox West Coast fashion—backed by extravagantly styled contemporary decor—a tantalizing variety of oversized candy treats, soft drinks, ice cream, and even packaged hot nuts joined popcorn in coercing moviegoers to part with their loose change. (AMPAS.)

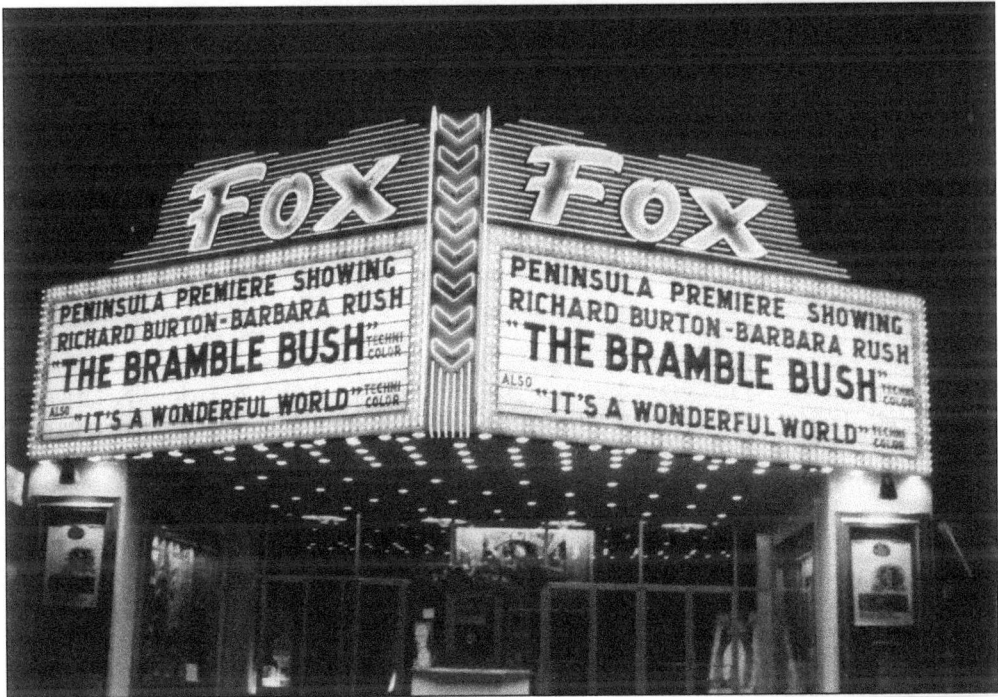

The remodeled Peninsula reopened as the Fox on August 23, 1957; this 1960 photograph shows it in all its nighttime neon grandeur. A new marquee and ticket lobby were built along lines typical of many remodels done throughout the Fox West Coast circuit at the time. As the years went on, decreasing attendance and increasing overhead had the inevitable results. The lights would be turned off for the last time on September 14, 1974. The Fox Mall now occupies the site. (AMPAS.)

The Broadway, located at 1157 California Drive just south of Broadway, opened on March 25, 1930. It was Burlingame's second large theater, about half the size of the Peninsula, which had opened three and a half years earlier (pages 40–43). It was traditionally a second-run house, offering films that had already premiered downtown, but still had some mileage in them, or titles that the Peninsula chose to bypass. (AMPAS.)

Bond-selling promotions were a major patriotic effort during World War II. The double feature of *Dillinger* and *Betrayal From the East* is typical of what wartime action audiences were seeking and getting. This photograph shows the elaborate neon fenestration, which had been added to the original marquee when the Broadway was less than 10 years old. The Broadway was the work of the prolific Reid Bros. architectural firm. (AMPAS.)

James and Merritt Reid knew how to provide grandeur and economy. Much of the auditorium was structural concrete painted in imitation of stone blocks. Accents of plaster sculpture completed the look, with the grilles fronting the chambers housing the two-manual, six-rank Leathurby-Smith pipe organ being the most ornate features. With the advent of wide-screen movies, a new CinemaScope screen would be set in front of the proscenium arch. (AMPAS.)

The Broadway was renamed the Encore on April 21, 1965, and for the next decade attempted to establish itself as a repertory and revival house under the management of Ward F. Stoopes (1926–1999). The Taylor family installed a seven-rank Wurlitzer pipe organ at this time. But the operation did not last and finally closed in September 1975. In later years, it became a church and was demolished in the late 1990s.

Theater-in-the-round was a cultural phenomenon of the mid-1960s, particularly in suburbia. The Hyatt Music Theatre, located at 1304 Bayshore Highway in Burlingame, burst upon the scene with a maximum of fanfare on September 5, 1964, with Pat Suzuki in *The Flower Drum Song*. It was followed by such mouthwatering (at least on paper) attractions as Ginger Rogers in *Annie Get Your Gun*, Janet Blair in *The Sound of Music*, Howard Keel in *South Pacific*, Kathryn Grayson and Dorothy Dandridge in *Show Boat*, and Tammy Grimes in *Finian's Rainbow*. The Hyatt Music

Theatre cost $2.5 million, had 2,500 seats, and boasted that no ticket holder would be more than 60 feet from the stage. Big-name stars appeared; most were well established as Hollywood headliners but with their glory days behind them. Original New York cast members, such as Suzuki and Grimes, reprised their original roles. With sure-fire Broadway shows that had by than become part of the popular American musical culture, how could they go wrong? But they did. In less than two years, the bubble had burst, and it was all over.

Theatre-in-the-round was a concept suited best to concert performances by individual artists who could use the round stage and close proximity to the audience to their advantage. Staging actual productions was another matter. Players had to make their entrances and exits running up and down the aisles, and scenery had to be changed in full view of the audience during lengthy intermissions. Technological glitches were so common that audiences often felt they were witnessing a Marx Brothers production akin to *A Night at the Opera*. To San Francisco–based theatergoers accustomed to high levels of professionalism at the Geary, the Curran, and the War Memorial Opera House, it was all a bad joke. To the Hollywood and New York professionals who found themselves trapped beneath dangling microphones over the circular center stage, it was an embarrassment—their tarnished reputations sinking in the mire of disaster. Only 15 months after its arc-light opening, Hyatt Music Theatre offered its final presentation: Kathryn Crosby in *Peter Pan*. But there is more to the Hyatt's story.

Floundering in debt, the theater bravely attempted to reinvent itself as Hyatt Cinema, extensively remodeled into a single-screen theater by Syufy Enterprises and reopened on March 29, 1966, with the peninsula premiere of *Those Magnificent Men in Their Flying Machines*. Just six years later, the auditorium was split in half, and it reopened on December 6, 1972, as the Hyatt Twin. On October 12, 1984, it reopened once again, this time as a tri-plex. On October 5, 2006, Cinemark took over operation of Syufy Enterprises, and a few months later, on April 20, 2007, Hyatt closed its doors for the last time. Its equipment and furnishings were removed the following day, and it now stands vacant, awaiting its future. One can only imagine the amount of money lost at this site by a half century of optimistic entrepreneurs.

The Burlingame & Peninsula Twin Drive-In opened at 350 Beach Road, just off Airport Boulevard in Burlingame, on June 23, 1965, with a total capacity of 1,500 cars. Sharing a common box office, each screen had its own name, identity, and entrance, which probably seemed like a good idea in those early days of multiplexing. But it soon caused endless confusion, starting with its name and location and ending with drivers who found themselves on the wrong entrance ramp too late to change lanes. On November 16, 1973, it reopened with two more screens and officially became, quite simply, the Burlingame 4. It closed in 2001 and disappeared from view in 2002.

Hart's Theatre at 248 B Street in San Mateo is the earliest documented film venue in the area, opening around 1912. This rare image captures not only a perfect shot of the theater but also an idyllic view of B Street as it appeared nearly a century ago. The new medium of motion pictures proved one of the most popular technological innovations of the era, and within the next few years Roy's Theatre at 219 California Drive (1913), the Regent Theatre on San Mateo Drive at Baldwin (1915–1927), and the Garden Theatre at 1200 Burlingame Avenue (1918–1926, burned 1991) also threw their hats in the ring. Their success led to the opening of the magnificent San Mateo Theatre (next page) in 1925, but unable to compete with their immeasurably grander and newer neighbor, it was not long before they all disappeared and were soon forgotten.

Architects Irving F. Morrow and William I. Garren designed a spectacular and unusual showplace for San Mateo. Somewhat Spanish in style, it also contained numerous modern design elements. The auditorium walls were painted structural concrete, and exposed wooden planking made up the ceiling. The proscenium arch and grilles fronting the two-manual, eight-rank Leathurby-Smith organ evidenced the Spanish style. The patterning of the grilles, mural work over the proscenium, and fabric wall hangings along the sides were thoroughly modern. No theater thus decorated had yet been built. The San Mateo could lay claim to being the first American theater to be partially ornamented in what is now called Art Deco. (Theatre Historical Society of America.)

The San Mateo Theatre, at 66 Third Avenue, opened on July 23, 1925, with a seating capacity of 1,215, the first of three extraordinary new structures in the Mid-Peninsula devoted to the presentation of motion pictures. It was followed by the Peninsula in Burlingame (pages 40–43) in 1926 and the Sequoia in Redwood City (pages 72–79). The facade gave few hints of the decorative innovations within; nevertheless, it was unusual. Tuscan and Greek details were combined with oversized Spanish elements. The facade of the auditorium block was studded with hundreds of cast concrete scallop shells. Morrow and Garren designed only one other theater, the Portal (now the CineArts Empire) in San Francisco. Irving Morrow and his wife, Gertrude, later gained fame with the design of the Golden Gate Bridge, including the selection of International Orange as its color. (Theatre Historical Society of America.)

Snack bars were an innovation of the 1940s, providing theaters with a new source of revenue and profit that had been untapped in previous years. Positioned so that they were the first thing patrons encountered when they entered the lobby and staffed by smiling, uniformed attendants, their immediate popularity raised the inevitable question, "Why didn't we think of something like this sooner?" (AMPAS.)

During the mid- to late 1930s, marquees were updated to conform to the ever-changing styles of the times. In this 1945 photograph, the San Mateo is still sporting its attractive prewar look with a neon-festooned marquee design that proliferated in the Fox West Coast chain. After nearly a half century of service to the community, the San Mateo closed permanently on February 10, 1974, and is now an office and retail building.

The Manor Theatre, located at 32 Twenty-fifth Avenue in San Mateo, opened on November 14, 1941, with a capacity of 984 stadium-style seats. Its trademark was its complex neon, dutifully maintained in later years by staff member Wally Hagaman. The architect was Frederick Quandt. After shutting down for remodeling, it reopened on April 9, 1975, as the Manor I & II, with separate auditoriums upstairs and downstairs. Just eight years later, it closed on April 17, 1983.

Save for the removal of the sign tower and marquee, the facade of the Manor looks much the same in this 1992 photograph as it did in its movie days. The interior was gutted to the bare walls, its circular lobby and auditorium murals reduced to rubble. Ironically, Mark Santa Maria, one of the demolition workers involved with removing the auditorium floor, later became interested in saving and restoring architectural elements from theaters. (Gary Lee Parks.)

Los Angeles architect S. Charles Lee began his career designing some of the finest movie theaters in Southern California in his late 20s. A handful of Bay Area theaters bore his stamp as well; San Mateo's Baywood was one. In this lobby view, ceiling decorations prove that even California's coastal oak leaves and acorns can be interpreted in Art Deco style. Etched glass chandeliers are identical to those found in Lee's theaters in Los Angeles.

S. Charles Lee gave the moviegoers of San Mateo as much Hollywood glitz as his client's budget allowed, bringing Los Angeles decorator Anthony B. Heinsbergen's painters to cover walls and ceilings with a riot of sun rays, swirling clouds, and zigzags. A pair of classical statues, ornamental ventilation grilles, and a few gilded plaster scrolls and curls were some of the few three-dimensional details included in the design of the theater.

The Baywood, located at 359 B Street in San Mateo, opened on August 20, 1931. It was San Mateo's second major motion picture venue, with a seating capacity of 1,081. By the 1950s, the impact of television, difficulty of parking, and competition from drive-ins so impacted its income that it ceased to be a profitable operation. It closed on April 26, 1953, and was gutted for reuse as a Thrifty drug store. Today, the building is vacant, save for an independent bookstore in one portion of the space. Above the drug store's dropped ceiling, angled steel beams from the balcony structure can still be found along with sections of the auditorium murals, which show that in the 1940s scenes of trees and flowers were painted over the original Art Deco geometric patterns. High above these, a few ornamental plaster steps and curls cling to the structural concrete. The fortress-like facade still exists behind the drugstore fascia, and there has been talk of revealing it as part of a remodeling of the building.

The Palm, located at 1705 Palm Avenue, was San Mateo's fourth indoor theater of the modern era. It opened on March 10, 1950, with 750 seats. Its intention was to provide a second-run neighborhood venue to augment the city's three larger first-run theaters. There was an attempt at foreign films when it operated as the Paris in 1950–1951. In June 1972, it made the plunge into "adult" programming—its trademark for the next 30 years. It closed in 2005 and was torn down.

General Cinema's Hillsdale Cinema, located at 3011 El Camino Real in San Mateo, opened on December 23, 1966; it was twinned and reopened on November 19, 1971, and later converted into a four-plex in July 1981. As the auditoriums got smaller, so did the audiences. It closed on December 1, 1998, and was converted into a home accessories store. Around the back of the building, the large structure that housed the movie speakers can still be seen.

The Century 12, located at 320 Second Avenue in San Mateo, opened on February 7, 2003. A Neo-Moderne vertical sign announces the theater's presence to passersby, and a long courtyard leads patrons to the entrance, which is tastefully patterned to blend with the many Art Deco commercial buildings in the downtown area. By the year 2000, it was widely accepted in new cinema design to do away with the stark simplicity of early multiplexes in favor of giving at least a nod to the architectural showmanship of the past.

Fashion Island Cinema 6 opened on November 25, 1981, on Fashion Island in Foster City, an engineered landfill in the marshes of San Francisco Bay on the eastern edge of San Mateo. The shopping center in which it was located was never successful, and one by one the anchors closed, so in later years it resembled a ghost town. The shoebox six-plex closed on September 4, 1995, after which the entire shopping center was torn down. The retail complex on the site today bears an Art Deco Revival look, far more suggestive of theatricality than the actual cinema that preceded it, even though the new development has no theater.

Belmont's first theater, the Starlite Drive-In on Ralston Avenue, opened on September 19, 1947, as a sister to the similarly named Starlite Drive-In in South San Francisco (pages 24–25). On October 19, 1949, Belmont's first indoor enterprise, built by Roy Cooper of West Valley Theatres, opened at 100 El Camino Real, its towering vertical sign a beacon welcoming visitors to the community. In the mid-1960s, the former carpet store next door was converted into the Bel-Art, specializing in imported film fare. In this sense, it became the first twin operation in the area. In 1972, the two theaters began to run as a single operation, the Belmont I & II under the Cooper banner. In 1977, the original auditorium was cut in half, creating what was now identified as the Belmont Cinemas Three. At this time, its original crimson walls and trademark swirling floral mural patterns were draped over, never to be seen again. After Cooper's death, operation passed from one organization to another, and the Belmont closed in 1997. It is now a fitness center.

The Carlos Theatre, at 1224 San Carlos Avenue, celebrated its invitational grand opening on January 10, 1941, and opened to the public the following evening. S. Charles Lee designed it as a stunning Moderne showplace for his clients, Fox West Coast Theatres. The late 1930s ushered in a look for theaters long since called the Skouras style after Fox's head of exhibition, Charles P. Skouras. The decor made use of oversized swirling floral patterns executed in gilded cast plaster, paint, or both. While not exclusive to new or remodeled Fox theaters of the late 1930s to the mid-1950s, it was in that chain's venues that the style was chiefly popularized. Designer Carl G. Moeller was the man behind the look, likely working hand in hand with the architect on each job. In this photograph, it is possible to see the kind of lighting that decorated the streets of America before energy crises and the earth-toned 1970s put an end to the fun.

Plans for a major movie theater in San Carlos had been discussed as early as the 1920s. By 1940, when the Carlos was built, parking had already become a major concern, and forward-looking site planners saw to it that plenty of room was provided. In this remarkable aerial view, about 200 parking spaces surround the Carlos Theatre and the adjoining Bank of America. The words "San Carlos" are sprawled across the roof of the theater, a landmark to passing airplanes.

In this 1945 image of the then five-year-old Carlos, one of architect S. Charles Lee's signature custom box office designs can be seen. It is finished in polished metal and etched glass, and its flanks are paneled in marble with patterns sandblasted into them. Careful scrutiny of the original photograph reveals posted admission prices: 20¢ for children, 45¢ for juniors, 60¢ for adults, and 85¢ for loge seating. (AMPAS.)

The flamboyant, 727-seat Carlos auditorium is pictured in classic Skouras style. Sculpted leaf forms around the screen were finished with a gold-colored metal alloy. Under the illumination of the houselights, the walls were cream, the large circles were crimson, and the leafy swirls were in tones of green. When the lights went down, ultraviolet lamps hidden in the bowl-shaped wall fixtures caused all the painted patterns to glow. (AMPAS.)

Rain often acted like a magnet bringing people out to see a movie. Esther Williams and Red Skelton in *Texas Carnival* (misspelled on marquee) show what star power was about on a wintry afternoon in December 1951. Both features were in Technicolor. The design of the trapezoidal marquee was used on several Fox West Coast theaters in cities as near as San Francisco and as far away as Watsonville and Bakersfield.

By 1973, the Carlos was still a major player, here offering a great double bill of two wildly popular science fiction films of that year: *Westworld* and *Soylent Green*. The Bank of America next door had become Eureka Federal Savings. But three years later, on September 14, 1976, the Carlos would close its doors forever, replaced by what would be Eureka's new headquarters. Eureka sponsored a nostalgic movie night for the public before demolishing all buildings on the block.

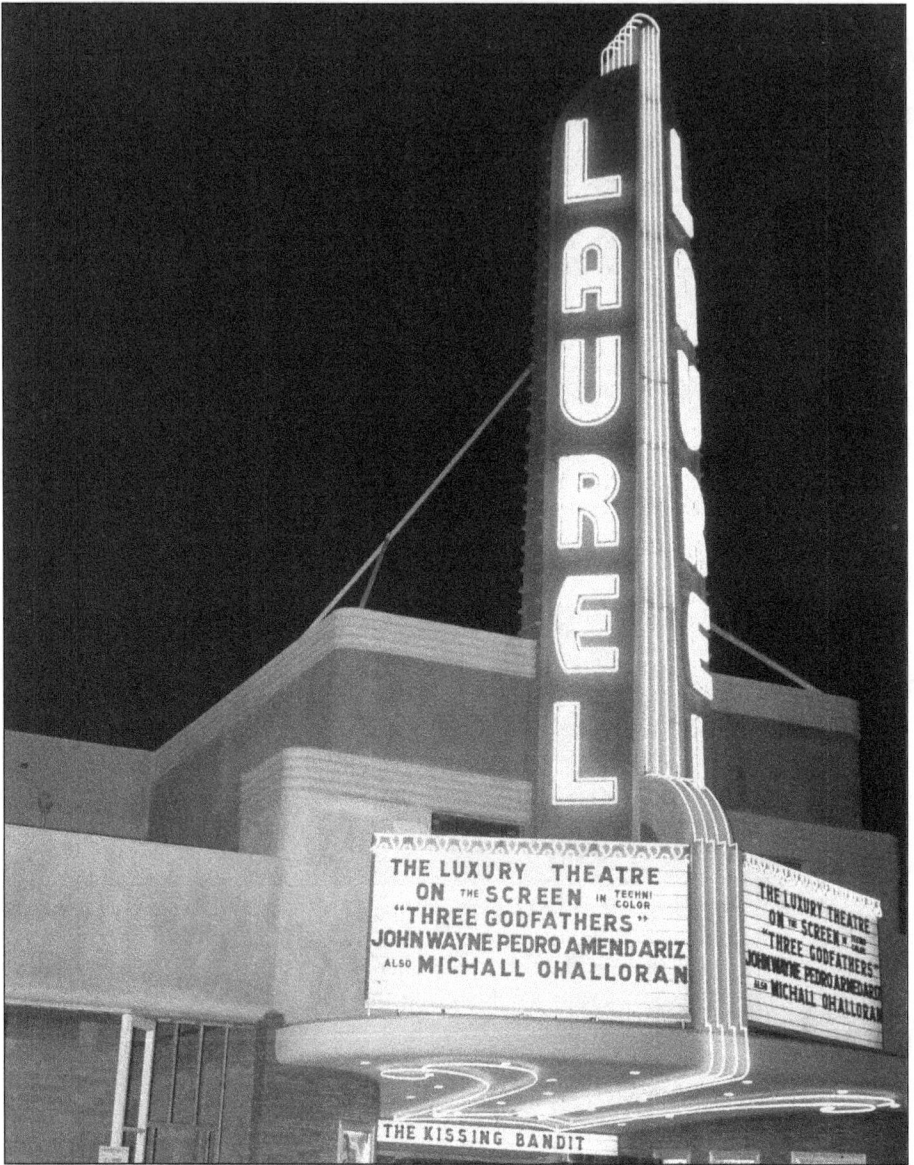

The Laurel Theatre, at 1500 Laurel Street in San Carlos, opened on February 19, 1949, one of the first postwar theaters to be completed at a time when moviegoing was at its peak. Frederick W. Quandt was the architect. The Laurel's sign tower spelled the theater's name on three sides, though the backside was less brightly lit out of consideration for nearby homes. The letters facing Laurel Street, however, were outlined in neon and filled with hundreds of bright, incandescent bulbs. The tower was a necessary beacon to traffic on El Camino Real. Nevertheless, because of declining attendance, it drifted into adult films in the 1970s, a less than welcome bill of fare on the conservative downtown San Carlos menu. Following a final blaze of glory as a general audience theater around the turn of the decade, the Laurel closed on July 31, 1985. An impassioned attempt by a very small band of residents to save the theater was made in the mid-1990s, but the demolition crew came in January 1998. The developer's drawings of the condominiums planned for the site showed the retention of the Laurel's signature sign tower, and the letters were carefully removed, but the tower never reappeared on the finished development.

Coming the better part of a decade after crosstown competitor the Carlos, the Laurel was sleeker and less flamboyant, yet the theater was still part of the show. Flexwood paneling, a planter box, tropically inspired mural work, and a brass-and-crystal-bead chandelier offer modernistic luxury. A drinking fountain on the far wall has a taller fount for adults in the center and two smaller founts on either side for children. (AMPAS.)

By the time the Laurel's 900-seat auditorium was designed, formulas had been established by decorators for theater interiors. It is possible to find identical painted designs in different theaters. In this case, the same tropical natives found on the walls of the Laurel appeared on the walls of the Stamm Theatre in Antioch. Ultraviolet bulbs illuminated the murals in both theaters. The Laurel was "cooled by refrigeration," a climate-controlled luxury in the Bay Area. (AMPAS.)

The Tivoli Theatre, at 716 Laurel Street in San Carlos, opened on May 19, 1965. It was owned and operated by Edgar Sutro, who had already found success at the Bijou in Palo Alto (page 110). A decade later, on October 8, 1975, it reopened as the Tivoli Twin. It closed in 1982. Soon after closing, the building was given a more decorative facade treatment and was christened the Tivoli Building. Today, it houses offices on a second floor, and a large restaurant on the street level welcomes the public from beneath a canopy that looks more like a theater marquee than anything the building had during its movie years.

The Circle Star Theatre, located at 2 Circle Star Way in San Carlos, opened on October 13, 1964, with Jane Powell in *My Fair Lady*. Similar in design, construction, and programming to the Hyatt Music Theatre (pages 46–49), it faced most of the same problems the Hyatt did. Marquee Entertainment purchased it in 1971 and brought it back to life by booking an incredible variety of big-name acts, such as Frank Sinatra, Marlene Dietrich, Perry Como, and Judy Garland, and Motown acts to increase its diversity. Its complete roster of entertainers reads like a who's who in popular music of the last half of the 20th century, seen to advantage on a circular stage that actually revolved in both directions. In later years, newer entrepreneurs were not so lucky, and declining attendance brought about its final closure in December 1993. After standing vacant for several years, the building caught fire in 1997 and was demolished. The Circle Star Center, comprising two office buildings and a small hotel, now stands on the site. The steel frame of the marquee fronting the Bayshore Freeway was restyled to support a pair of animated LED billboards. Three of the original crystal-beaded wall fixtures from the Circle Star are displayed at the local history museum.

It is appropriate for Redwood City, San Mateo's county seat, to boast what is believed to be the county's first theater. The Alhambra opened on Main Street in 1896 and still stands today, commemorated by a plaque identifying its history. As with many playhouses of the 19th century, the auditorium was perched over storefronts, and windows were provided in the front and sidewalls for added illumination. (Redwood City Public Library History Room.)

The great San Francisco earthquake of April 18, 1906, also shook Redwood City and severely damaged the Alhambra. Here, a portion of the auditorium sidewall has crushed an adjacent business, but the theater's facade stands firm. The Alhambra's exterior was an early example of the Mission Revival style that would take hold in California and remain popular in varying forms to the present day. (Redwood City Public Library History Room.)

The Princess nickelodeon opened on Main Street near the Masonic hall and the rebuilt Alhambra Theatre in the first decade of the 20th century. To polish the image of movies as a cultured form of entertainment, prefabricated cast plaster elements utilized to build attractive entrances (such as the one shown) were available from mail order catalogs. The unidentified young gentleman in this 1909 photograph is most likely both manager and projectionist. (Redwood City Public Library History Room.)

In 1910, two more movie theaters opened in Redwood City: the Lyric, a nickelodeon on Broadway, and the Bell (not pictured), on Main Street. Theatres came and went quickly in those fledgling years of movie exhibition, and name changes were common, but their popularity knew no bounds. The no-nonsense wooden front of the Lyric would sport a new name—the Gem—before it vanished in favor of more handsome structures. (Redwood City Public Library History Room.)

Ellis J. Arkush, who had taken over the Bell nickelodeon on Main Street, opened the Sequoia Theatre on Broadway at Jefferson Street in 1916. It was a steel-reinforced concrete structure, and while equipped with a small stage, its narrow auditorium was clearly designed for movies. Faced with a marquee worthy of any high-class theater, it would operate until the opening of Arkush's new Sequoia in 1929. (Redwood City Public Library History Room.)

Today, few people passing by this innocuous, vacant building at 2116 Broadway would suspect that 90 years ago it was Redwood City's leading motion picture emporium, the popular center of attraction in the photograph above. In the intervening years, it served as a downtown bank and other purposes, but now it seems to have reached a dead end. (Gary Lee Parks.)

Inspired by Gothic architecture from Europe, Ellis Arkush commissioned San Francisco's Reid Bros. to design a block-wide theater, office, and retail complex on Broadway across from the county courthouse. The $300,000 new Sequoia Theatre building was quite modern in its almost skyscraper-like use of vertical lines. Here, management and staff pose below the marquee whose lightbulb-clad "SEE" and "HEAR" signage atop the theater's name announces the arrival of the talkies. (Redwood City Public Library History Room.)

To be a theater usher was a dream of many an American boy during the 1920s and 1930s. The job demanded efficiency and courtesy. To be seen in a well-pressed uniform by one's peers was coveted. These young men are posing outside the auditorium wall in 1931. The gentleman in the double-breasted jacket was likely the doorman. (Redwood City Public Library History Room.)

By late 1933, less than five years after it had opened, the dark days of the Great Depression had taken their toll on the Sequoia. The illuminated 25¢ admission price over the marquee—larger than the combined titles of both films being shown on the double-feature program—says it all.

A decade later and with an updated marquee, the financially prosperous moviegoing days of World War II have once again brightened the Sequoia's prospects, as seen in this 1945 photograph. The marquee shown is the same one that exists today, save for a different neon-lettered name (next page).

As originally designed, the Sequoia's auditorium was atmospheric with faux Spanish village facades parading beneath a plaster sky. On June 21, 1950, at 11:30 p.m., during a showing of *The Gunfighter*, the sky fell, causing injury to 27 patrons in the balcony. The collapse was blamed on over 20 years of vibrations from passing trains. (Redwood City Public Library History Room.)

On September 15, 1950, three months after the collapse, the Sequoia, now rechristened the Fox and its seating reduced from 1,464 to 1,325, hosted a grand reopening celebration, which became a big-time Redwood City event. "Movies are Better Than Ever," was Hollywood's slogan of the year, its first visible gesture of defiance against the looming specter of competition from television.

Two generations of young Saturday matinee moviegoers celebrated the end of the school week with a trip to their local movie theater. Features, comedy shorts, cartoons, and the camaraderie of friends were enhanced by plenty of popcorn and other treats. In the fall of 1956, a double feature of *It Conquered the World* and *The She Creature* was just about as good as it got. (AMPAS.)

An interior tour of the Fox begins. The entryway was completely remodeled in the so-called Skouras style. The neon on the ceiling above the prefabricated box office of aluminum and molded fiberglass matched the swirls of a multicolored terrazzo sidewalk below. The admission prices ranged from 90¢ for adults, $1.10 for loge seating, 70¢ for juniors, and 35¢ for children. (AMPAS.)

Here is a view of the Fox grand lobby from the mezzanine. The Gothic-inspired vaulted ceiling, classical pilasters, and murals of trees were left from the original design of the theater. New patterns were added to all of the ceilings, and mirrored panels covered a wall over the entrance doors. Chandeliers were retrofitted with new ornaments in brass sheet metal wrought to resemble leaves. (AMPAS.)

The entrance doors looked through the grand lobby to an inner lobby on the main floor and a wide mezzanine promenade above. The wrought-iron railings and the ornate plasterwork accents remained from the 1929 decor of the theater's Sequoia days, and they harmonized well with the 1950 Skouras additions. Velvet drapes softened the room aesthetically and acoustically, as did thick floral-patterned carpeting. (AMPAS.)

To restore public faith in the theater after the collapse of the original ceiling, the auditorium was completely overhauled. This photograph dates to the 1980s. By this time, some of the drapes had been removed, showing that underneath the oversized gilded floral plasterwork, the original proscenium and organ grilles were still extant, as well as the original mural fire-safety curtain.

Wide-screen CinemaScope, initially unveiled in the fall of 1953, was Hollywood's answer of defiance to small-screen television, which had seriously deflated moviegoing attendance by this time. The Fox was blessed with a stage wide enough to handle this new medium as it was meant to be seen with the added impact of four-track magnetic stereophonic sound. (AMPAS.)

In this 2010 photograph, the exterior of the Fox building stands in a nearly restored condition. In previous years, the theater continued with first-run movies. With the arrival of competition from multiplexes, it exhibited adult film fare for a time and then found use as an auction house, followed by new life as a home for stage productions. In the new millennium, local real estate businessman John Anagnostou brought a variety of top-name live music acts to the Fox, giving the stage a much needed upgrading, while beginning a program to restore extensive ornamental detailing that had been removed from the exterior over the years. Now under the stewardship of new owner Eric Lochtefeld, the Fox still soldiers on. Here, carefully refurbished storefronts on the corner of Broadway and Theatre Way await the hoped-for return to a better retail climate. (Gary Lee Parks.)

The Redwood Theatre on the corner of James Avenue and Winklebleck Street opened on June 3, 1933, with a live performance by banjoist Eddie Peabody and a screen presentation of *Be Mine Tonight*. By the mid-1940s, it called itself the Little Theatre of Big Pictures, but its film fare consisted mostly of B-level programmers—often Westerns, and last-run biggies—until its closure in 1955. A Bank of America branch was built on the site, which now houses an auto-parts store.

The Redwood's design was yet another opus by Los Angeles architect S. Charles Lee. While oftentimes an innovative designer, he was also capable of designing for clients on a tight budget, and his concept for the Redwood fit the bill. A look at the auditorium shows an attempt to give the boxy interior some of the same plaster and paint undulations characteristic of Lee's celebrated work in the Los Angeles basin. (AMPAS.)

The Redwood Drive-In, at 557 East Bayshore Boulevard in Redwood City, opened on June 14, 1961, with a capacity of 1,300 cars. Built by Syufy Enterprises of San Francisco, the theater's architect was Vincent G. Raney, and its structural engineers were Pregnoff & Matheu. Its screen measured 90 feet in height and 130 feet in width, claiming to be the tallest outdoor movie screen in the world. The screen was elevated 30 feet off the ground for maximum viewing.

The backside of the Redwood screen, which framed its marquee, was prominently visible on the busy Bayshore Freeway night and day, providing instant identification of the site and the names of the films playing to thousands of passing motorists. By January 1976 when this photograph was taken, fast-buck titles like *Teenage Tramp* and *Confessions of a Window Cleaner* had already invaded the celluloid environment, for better or for worse, depending on the point of view. (CinemaTour.)

Originally a single screener, by the mid-1970s the Redwood had expanded to four screens. A total of three box office stations provided six lanes of entry, each with its own mini-marquee announcing the name of the film that would greet patrons once they were comfortably parked in one of the fields beyond—provided they had paid attention and gotten in the correct lane to start with. (CinemaTour.)

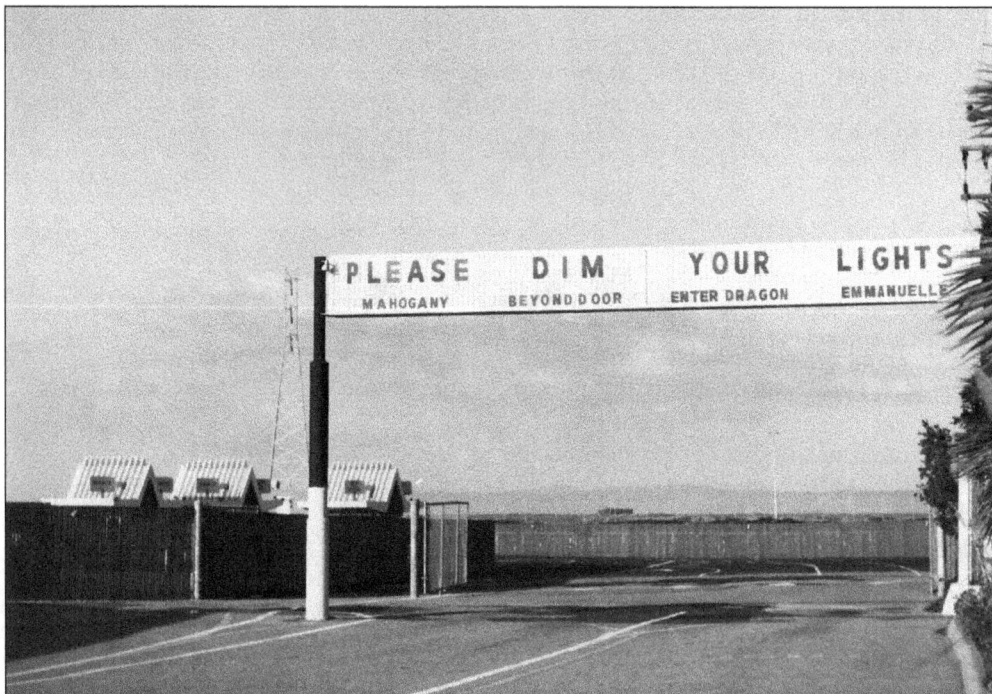

"PLEASE DIM YOUR LIGHTS" is not the name of a film, but a plea to drivers to turn off their headlights and switch to parking lights while entering the grounds. Noncompliance was met with the honking of horns by momentarily blinded moviegoers already positioned in front of the screen. This only made things worse, but it was part of the ritual. (CinemaTour.)

Patrons were encouraged to come early for the obvious reason of avoiding bottleneck lines at the box office, but also so the kids could have time to enjoy the playground—a fixture of drive-ins in a less litigious society. During the summer months, when the actual movies could not begin until the sun went down, some sites like the Redwood became mini-amusement parks in the early evening hours. And, of course, there was the snack bar. (CinemaTour.)

The massive cinder-block snack bar was, in reality, a fast-food restaurant yielding enormous profits to counteract the equally enormous overhead of operating these venues. Alongside the snack bar, a cinder-block cubicle housed the projection equipment required to animate the giant screen beyond. This was not an enviable job, considering the heat of summer, the cold of winter, and all the inherent mechanical problems that came with the territory. (CinemaTour.)

The interior of the Redwood snack bar offers a rare glimpse into the heart and soul of drive-in theaters during the peak of their popularity. A tempting array of tasty and nutritious treats greets the eye of the hungry, but indecisive, buyer. Shall it be pizza (six varieties to choose from), a hot tamale, a hamburger or cheeseburger, a hotdog or a corn dog, or perhaps, a hot sandwich (ingredients unspecified)? Intermissions between films lasted from 15 to 20 minutes, and four check stands, each with its own cash register, insured that everyone was accommodated with maximum efficiency. Although just a simple cinder-block structure, the snack bar's floors were maintained with a sparkling polish. (CinemaTour.)

The enormity of drive-ins like the Redwood, which were typical of their era, is hard to comprehend. This aerial view, taken in the summer of 1982, gives an idea of the amount of acreage involved. Adjoining industrial parks are dwarfed by comparison. The original screen is on the far right (to the west) next to the Bayshore Freeway, and three more screens have been added on the east side. The complex was served by two projection booths, each one strategically positioned so that cars could face only one screen at a time. (CinemaTour.)

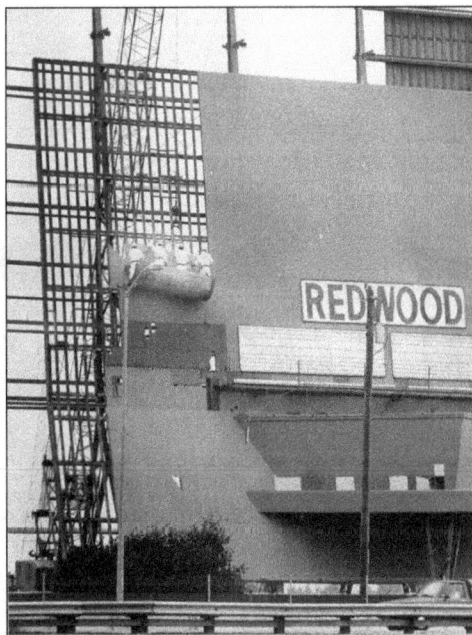

The Redwood Drive-In closed on September 13, 1987, and Cleveland Wrecking Company was contracted to bring down the screen tower the following month. In this photograph by Ted Fink, taken on October 16, 1987, four workmen are seen peeling the sheet metal from the screen frame one piece at a time. The Century Park 12 (page 87) would open on the same site three years later; flash forward 18 years, and it too would be history. Time marches on! (Redwood City Public Library History Room.)

The UA Redwood City 6—six shoeboxes in search of an audience—opened May 14, 1982, at 305 Walnut Street. Like its many similarly designed brethren, it failed to attract audiences large enough to sustain the overhead of its operation, and it soon disappeared with no trace. Miscellaneous commercial structures now stand on the site.

Adult theaters were a trend of the 1970s and often reared their not-always-welcome heads in the most unlikely places despite intense local opposition. Redwood City's cinder-block Lily Theatre, located at 2821 El Camino Real, was a typical storefront operation, combining live shows with "hardcore live action adult motion pictures" from 10:00 a.m. until 2:00 a.m. Few tears were shed when it closed a decade later, a chapter of local history best left closed.

Nearly three years after the demise of the Redwood City Drive-In (pages 81–85), the Century Park 12, also designed by Vincent Raney, rose like a phoenix from its ashes and opened on the same site May 18, 1990. Like its sister theater in South San Francisco (page 36), it was a relatively short-lived operation that closed in 2006. As of this writing, the building is barricaded, and the parking lot is used by a local dealership for storing new cars.

With the 2006 opening of the Century 20 on Broadway and Theatre Way next to the refurbished Fox Theatre, moviegoing returned to downtown Redwood City. Decorated with Art Deco Revival–sculpted panels, and complete with a towering fin-like vertical sign reminiscent of theaters of decades past, the Century 20 has combined old-style sparkle with contemporary megaplex practicality. With the Century and the Fox standing side by side, a degree of nighttime excitement and economic vitality has returned to the city center. (Gary Lee Parks.)

Menlo Park's first theater, the Fremont, opened on January 19, 1918, on El Camino Real near Santa Cruz Avenue. Records indicate that it had 1,400 seats. It closed in 1921, later becoming Slinger's Garage, and was eventually torn down.

The first Menlo Theatre, located at 947 El Camino Real, opened in 1923 on the site presently occupied by the Guild (next page). In later years, it was remodeled and renamed the New Menlo, operated by Harvey Amusements. It closed on March 13, 1947, and was partially demolished to accommodate the widening of El Camino Real.

The interior of the former Menlo during its years as the Guild reflects the results of the remodeling with typical-of-the-era wall murals depicting the now-ubiquitous naked nymphs or demigods in pursuit of white unicorns, bulls, and other assorted wildlife for purposes incomprehensible to the moviegoers who sat in their midst.

Once El Camino Real was properly widened, it was time to build the Guild in what was left of the old Menlo shell; with 330 seats, it opened its doors on March 30, 1948, with Noel Coward's *This Happy Breed,* a popular British World War II cavalcade that did not reach this country's shores until three years later. Since that time, the Guild has remained Menlo Park's primary art-movie house and survives today as one of the few single-screen theaters still in operation.

In the 1960s, the Guild's murals were covered and the interior given a black and orange so-called Mod color scheme. During the years that the Guild was part of Bay Area exhibitor Allen Michaan's circuit, salvaged features from Richmond's Fox and San Francisco's Uptown Theatres were used to banish the 1960s decor to blessed oblivion. Today, few patrons are aware that they are watching movies in the shell of a much older theater, the former Menlo. (Martin Schmidt.)

Menlo Park's 800-seat Park opened on March 14, 1947, with *The Razor's Edge*, a prestigious American film of the era, and maintained its status as the city's leading celluloid venue for the next half century. It closed its doors for the last time on July 28, 2002, a victim of changing times and tastes; a bitter pill to swallow for its local citizenry, but goodwill alone is not enough to compensate for ever-increasing overhead and a nightly sea of empty seats.

Following its closure, the Park's vertical sign was stealthily torn from the facade early one Sunday morning in an attempt to prevent landmark designation. This ploy failed, and the city forbade any further alterations to the building. Since then, several proposals have surfaced: one would retain the facade and a restored sign as the front of a small office building; another would restore the theater as a dance studio and intimate performing-arts facility. But for now, locals must rely on memories and photographs to recall the Park's magenta and white neon display. (Martin Schmidt.)

The Burgess Theatre, at 601 Laurel Street opposite Burgess Park in Menlo Park, was the home of the Menlo Players Guild, a reputable local theater group that traced its roots back to 1940. The building was demolished in 2002 after a decision from the city not to retrofit the building, by that time considered potentially susceptible to earthquake damage, and the land on which it stood was reclaimed.

The latter-day Menlo, located at 635 Santa Cruz Avenue and Doyle Street, opened with much fanfare on April 9, 1969. Patrons attended an invitation premiere of *The Prime of Miss Jean Brodie*, which had just won Maggie Smith an Academy Award for Best Actress of the Year. After three separate management attempts, it closed permanently in September 1982. A restaurant has operated in the building ever since.

Replacing the Half Moon Bay Theatre on Main Street, the Patio Theatre, located at Miramontes and Purissima Streets in Half Moon Bay, opened in 1950 and was operated by Alvin and Harvey Hatch. The architect was Otto Deichmann. Ward Stoopes took over operation in 1956, Tesco Tesi and Robert Swift kept the projectors whirring in the 1960s, and Walt Von Houffe did the same in the early 1970s. Following closure in the mid-1970s, it was converted to the Camilla Court office complex. (Half Moon Bay Historical Society.)

In the 1940s, even the little coastal town of Pescadero merited a theater. During that decade, the 1890 Methodist Episcopal Church, by then (and since) used as the Native Sons of the Golden West Hall, did double duty as the Pescadero Theatre. The narthex was converted into a projection booth, a screen was installed in the former altar niche, and 150 patrons could be seated on the level wooden floor. Today, efforts are being made to fully restore the building as a multipurpose community facility. (Ed Weeks.)

Three

NORTHERN
SANTA CLARA COUNTY

Santa Clara County begins where San Mateo County ends and proceeds south through San Jose to Gilroy and beyond (see map on page 8). Since *Theatres of San Jose* has already covered San Jose and its surrounding communities, this survey here will only deal with the northernmost area, comprising Palo Alto, Mountain View, Los Altos, Sunnyvale, and Milpitas.

Palo Alto, home of Stanford University, will be the focus of attention. Here, one of the Peninsula's major theatrical venues, the Stanford Theatre, is alive and well thanks to David W. Packard's 1989 restoration. The authors are happy to provide a tasty array of images from its 85-year lifespan.

Pictured around 1911, H.C. Schmidt stands proudly in the auditorium of the Novelty Theatre, located at 185 University Avenue. The Novelty was built in 1893 when motion pictures were in their infancy, just an added attraction to the live vaudeville performances of the era. By 1909, the Novelty offered movies as its main attraction, the new technological marvel of the young 20th century. It closed on October 24, 1914, superseded by the bigger and better Varsity shown below.

The first Varsity, located at 263 University Avenue, opened on March 11, 1912, with a seating capacity of 525. For the next decade, it was Palo Alto's leading motion picture venue, an improvement over its predecessor, the Novelty (above), but it was soon to be outdistanced by the bigger and better Stanford, which would open in 1925. The Varsity closed July 6, 1927, but the name would soon loom over another marquee two months later. The first Varsity was divided down the middle, and today the building houses both a pizza parlor and an Asian noodle house.

The New Stanford Theatre, as it was originally known, opened on June 9, 1925, at 221 University Avenue. Designed by Weeks & Day and built at a cost of $300,000, it was the fifth link in a Peninsula theater chain operated by Ellis Arkush's Palo Alto Theatre Company. Arkush's holdings now included the Sequoia in Redwood City (page 72), the Garden in Burlingame, the Regent in San Mateo, and the Varsity in Palo Alto (preceding page), as well as the first Stanford also in Palo Alto, which closed when this one opened. The next link in the chain, the Peninsula in Burlingame (pages 40–43), was already under construction. The capacity of the New Stanford was quoted as 1,443, with 994 seats on the main floor and the remaining 449 in the loges and balcony.

In its decorative scheme—the work of Robert E. Powers Studio, collaborating closely with architects Charles Weeks and William Day—the New Stanford embraced a colorful blend of Greek and Assyrian styles. Here, in the mezzanine lounge, balcony support beams feature motifs derived from Greek vase paintings, and a pair of urns continues the theme. (AMPAS.)

After passing through a vaulted entrance vestibule, patrons found themselves in this grand lobby with a terra cotta floor, the work of San Jose manufacturer Solon & Schimmel Tile (S&S). Polychrome-glazed patterns decorated the staircase risers. False windows top the walls, and paired chimeras face off on the ceiling beams.

It is hard to imagine that Palo Alto's University Avenue of 85 years ago is the same thoroughfare familiar today. Only three parked cars are visible, and there is no traffic. Trolley tracks define the primary source of transportation. It could be Sunday morning with everyone at church. Facing east, the vertical sign of the New Stanford Theatre rises proudly on the north side of the street.

In this publicity photograph taken by Power studios, the balcony overlooks an orchestra pit large enough for several musicians, a piano, and the console of the three-manual, 10-rank Leathurby-Smith organ, played by organist-composer Elmer Vincent. Spaces between the sidewall tops and the faux wood-grain ceiling were painted and lit to resemble a twilight sky. (AMPAS.)

By late 1941 when this photograph was taken, the Stanford had moved along with the times and now reflected a contemporary image in keeping with the era. Since the early 1930s, its identity had been altered from New Stanford to Fox Stanford, and the original 1925 vertical sign had been removed, never to be replaced. A marquee with milk-glass letters lit from behind was the trademark of most major venues in the late 1930s. A giant banner, supplied by National Screen Service, proudly announced the name and players of the feature film. Parking places were neatly painted, but parking meters had not yet been introduced.

100

In this 1945 photograph, the marquee is typical of those retrofitted onto theaters in the 1930s. While all somewhat similar, each was given utmost care by the neon craftsmen, who heated and bent every glass tube by hand using patterns drawn on sheets of asbestos. The tubes were pumped with mixtures of neon and other gasses, creating a variety of colors.

Banners were often used over the exit doors to remind moviegoers what films were coming and flipped around to a similar position over the entrance doors once they were the current attraction. At the Stanford, likenesses of Hermes, Homer, Socrates, Sappho, and Demeter—added during a minor redecoration—look down with approval on the forthcoming arrival of *Salty O'Rourke* and *Bring on the Girls* in this 1945 photograph. (AMPAS.)

In mid-1956, like many of its Fox West Coast brethren, the Stanford received an overhaul. Filmgoers entered the lobby and were overwhelmed by the brightly illuminated etched-aluminum snack bar offering tasty treats—and a commensurate deluge of much needed profits to their purveyors. Bon-Bons were a popular ice cream item, and giant-sized Hershey bars epitomized high-calorie decadence. (AMPAS.)

A flurry of flags, a modernized and enlarged marquee, two sizes of red Bevelite letters announcing the attraction, and a string of moving neon arrows pointing in the direction of the box office typify mid-1950s moviegoing grandeur. But the freshly painted Greek masks, scrolls, and plume-like antefixae adorning the top of the facade link the site to its 1925 roots. (AMPAS.)

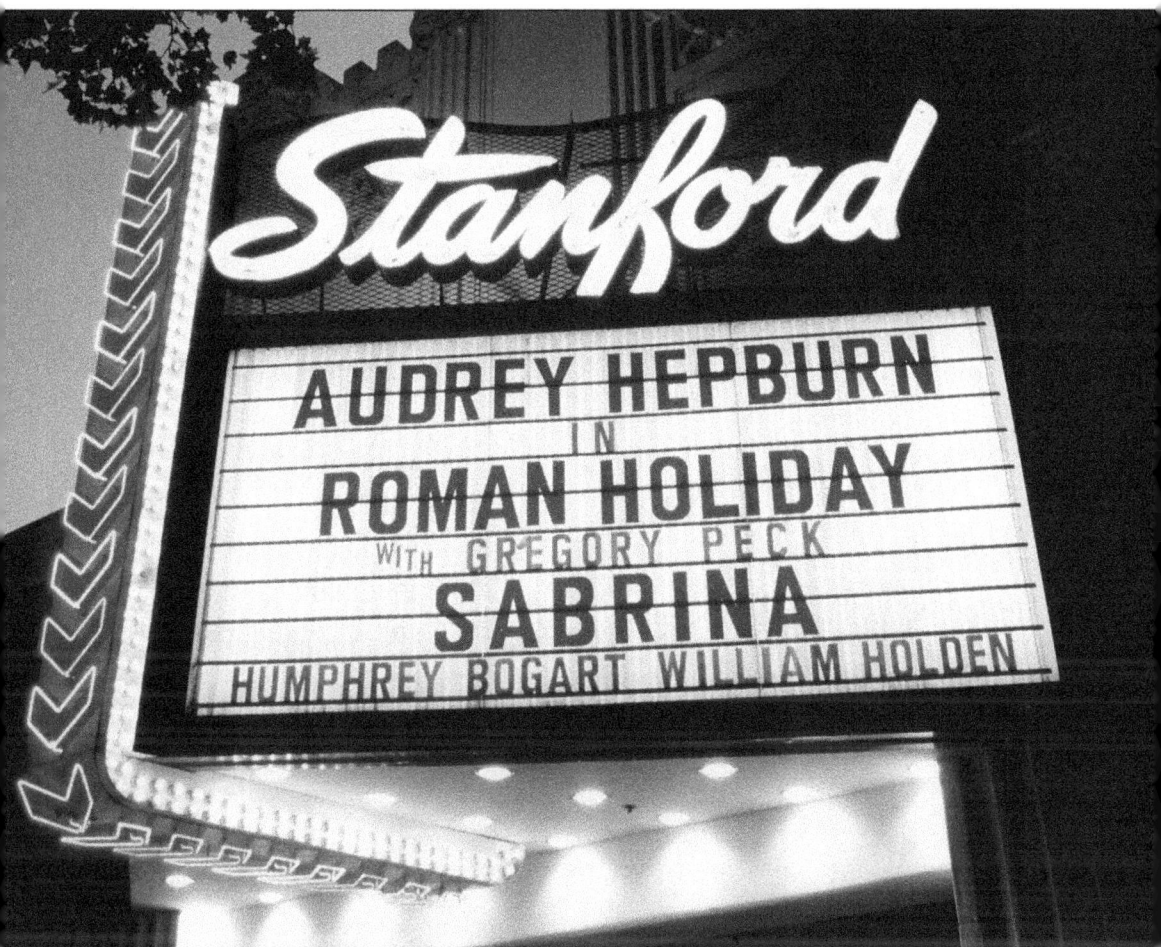

Following decades of operation under Fox West Coast and its successors, National General and Mann Theatres, the Stanford saw use as a legitimate playhouse in the 1980s, followed by one last turn as a first-run movie house under the Renaissance-Rialto banner. After presenting a six-week Fred Astaire festival, David W. Packard decided to purchase and restore the theater, reopening it in late 1989 as a full-time showcase for classic movies. A Wurlitzer organ, installed and maintained by Edward Millington Stout III and Dick Taylor, serenades the audience at intermission and gives voice to periodic silent film presentations. The Stanford Theatre Foundation dedicates itself to restoring and preserving classic motion pictures. In this 2002 photograph, the restored 1950s neon shines as brightly as ever. Beyond the doors, however, the theater replicates its 1925 appearance in nearly every respect, and a museum of posters and classic movie memorabilia occupies a former storefront next door. (Martin Schmidt.)

Palo Alto's second Varsity Theatre opened on September 27, 1927, at 456 University Avenue. Its signature Spanish-style courtyard was inspired partly by the successful courtyard entrance of Hollywood's Egyptian Theatre, but newspaper accounts of the time also cite the arches and columns of the Stanford University Quadrangle as having influenced architects James and Merritt Reid. The original color of the exterior imitated the authentic sandstone found at Stanford, but this was later repainted in white. The concrete pavement of the courtyard entry was stamped and tinted in multicolored pastel hues in imitation of irregular blocks of stone. A little fountain bubbled in its center. Once inside, patrons found a long, low-vaulted lobby, its ceiling beams painted in imitation of heavy wood and stenciled with heraldic shields, lions, scrolls, and garlands in hues of red, pale yellow, old rose, and gold. Wrought-iron chandeliers and wall sconces completed the look of Spanish baronial antiquity. The men's restroom was downstairs, beyond a columned niche fountain, but the women's was reached via a staircase and equipped with a spacious lounge that looked down at the courtyard. Once in the auditorium—which was at right angles to the lobby—patrons sat between arcaded sidewalls with cove-lit false windows and cornices topped with gilded shields and urns. An economical two-manual, seven-rank Leathurby-Smith organ held forth as the voice of the silent screen.

By 1942, the Varsity reflected the look of the late 1930s, much like that of the Stanford and several other sites already visited. Like the Broadway in Burlingame (pages 44–45), the Varsity served both as a move-over house for films that had already proven their popularity at the Stanford and still had mileage left in them and also as an outlet for lesser, often action-oriented fare that Fox West Coast considered unworthy of a Stanford playdate. The War Bond V for Victory kiosk out front was typical of its era, another example of theaters pitching in to do their share for the war effort, day and night.

In the 1950s, Fox West Coast was churning out their Skouras-styled snack bars like sausages. There must have been something in all that etched aluminum that stimulated the taste buds. With a smiling attendant ready to take an order, the Varsity offered a similar array of goodies. A jumbo box of popcorn sold for 10¢, as did a cup of Coca-Cola; profits were derived by volume, not by gouging, a lesson lost to today's money-hungry entrepreneurs.

By 1979 when this photograph was taken, the Varsity, independently operated by then, was leaning towards a student audience, as was the case of this Woody Allen double feature. The theater presented live folk, jazz, and rock concerts, an active repertory film schedule, a bar in the lobby, and a restaurant in the courtyard. After the demise of this creative and much-beloved operation, its final years were played out as a typical art-movie house under the Landmark banner. The Varsity permanently closed on July 8, 1994.

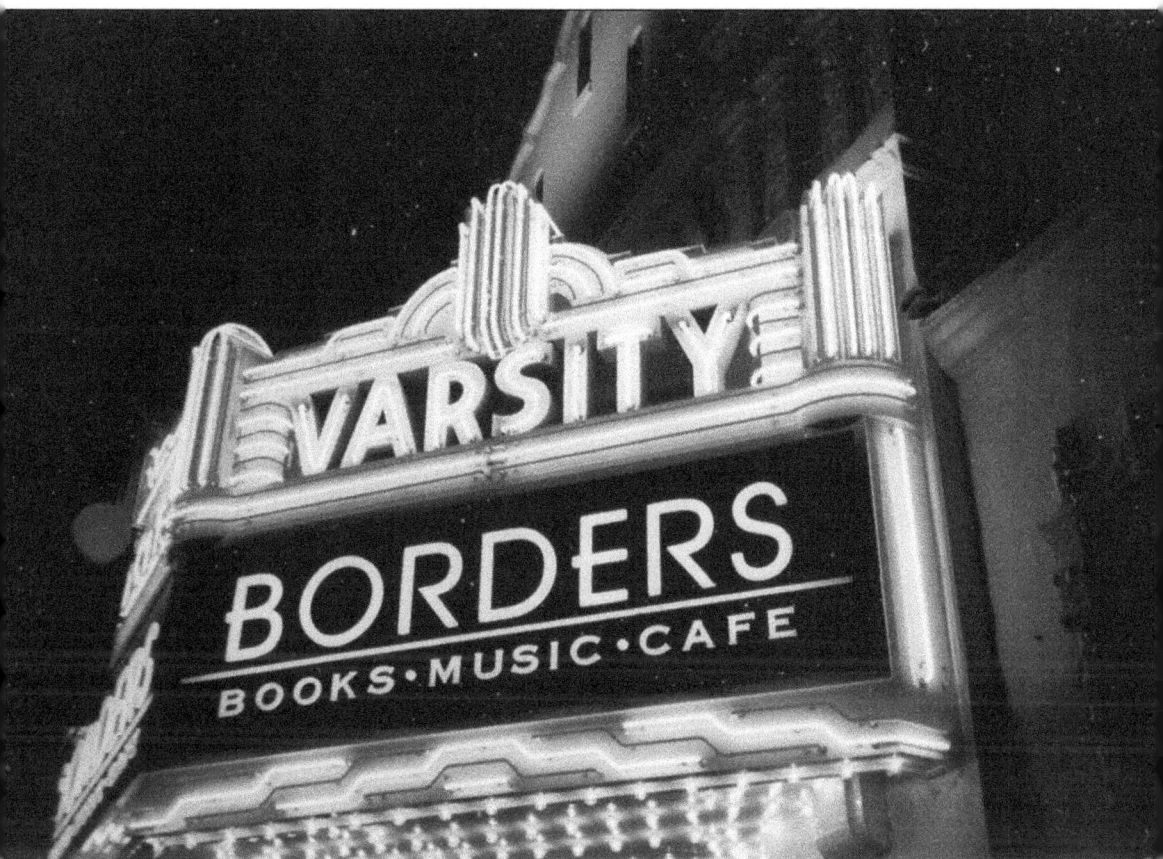

After a lengthy preservation battle, the Varsity, by now designated by the City of Palo Alto as an official historic site, underwent a massive redesign, emerging as Borders Books and Music while "preserving key historic elements," which in English meant saving the marquee, courtyard, lobby, auditorium ceiling, and parts of the interior sidewalls. (Gary Lee Parks.)

The California Theatre, at 427 California Avenue, opened on August 19, 1926, and was a medium-sized venue with 520 seats. A year later, it became known as Blanco's New California, a new member of the Blanco chain, and on June 12, 1936, was reopened as the Mayfield. Originally, the community of Mayfield was self-contained, but it was later annexed to Palo Alto.

On April 7, 1950, fire broke out at the Mayfield, causing extensive damage. Completely remodeled a year later, it reopened as the Cardinal, the address now being given as 429 California Avenue. Thanks in no small way to the Stanford University student population, moviegoing prospered in Palo Alto in the 1950s, and the Cardinal found its niche as a secondary house despite heavy competition from the Stanford and Varsity.

The California found its final and most successful identity when it was reopened as the Fine Arts on May 20, 1960, with the film version of Arthur Miller's *The Crucible*, shot in France three years earlier. It was the era of art and repertory, and for the next 25 years the Fine Arts was in the forefront. The theater closed October 25, 1987. Various retail uses have come and gone in the building, but the marquee still spells out the theater's name.

Edgar Sutro, who later opened the Tivoli in San Carlos (page 68), found immediate success in Palo Alto when he opened the Bijou, located at 640 Emerson Street, with the Palo Alto premiere of *Dr. Strangelove*, a hard act to follow in anybody's book. By the mid-1980s, it was all over, but there was new life to be found in such a desirable location, and it has since been the home of the Gordon Biersch Brewery.

The Festival Cinema, at 425 Hamilton Avenue, a haphazard attempt at repertory and revival, opened on December 15, 1972. Now primarily remembered as having beanbag chairs and mattresses strewn on the floor in front of the screen, it lasted over a decade and finally closed April 14, 1986. It is now a restaurant.

Palo Alto Square I & II, the area's second twin operation, opened on April 2, 1971, at 3000 El Camino Real. Now under Cinemark-Century Theatres control as Ciné Arts Palo Alto Square, its signature foliage-covered exterior is evergreen as ever. Popular among local moviegoers seeking foreign and independent film fare, only time will tell if the support of its fans is strong enough to subsidize its operation.

The Aquarius I & II, the area's first twin operation, opened on October 1, 1969, at 430 Emerson Street. Initially offering mainstream fare in direct competition with the Stanford around the corner, it soon found its niche as a site for foreign and independent films. From the beginning, political—or sometimes simply humorous—commentary on its marquee became its trademark, typified in this early nighttime image.

With seating capacities in the twin theater recently quoted as 235 and 145, and operated since 1985 by Landmark Theatres, the Aquarius offers an ideal situation for popular long-run attractions that fit nicely into the more intimate venue. A comparatively recent redecoration has added underwater-themed murals to the interior. One noteworthy accent is a friendly octopus perched high on the wall of the tiny lobby.

Los Altos, located at 200 Main Street in Los Altos, opened on May 18, 1949, and was designed by William David with William Wolf. To the casual observer, it looked like a spaceship from another planet—a bizarre, but unquestionably striking piece of aggressively modern architecture set in the midst of typical small-town business establishments. (Los Altos History Museum.)

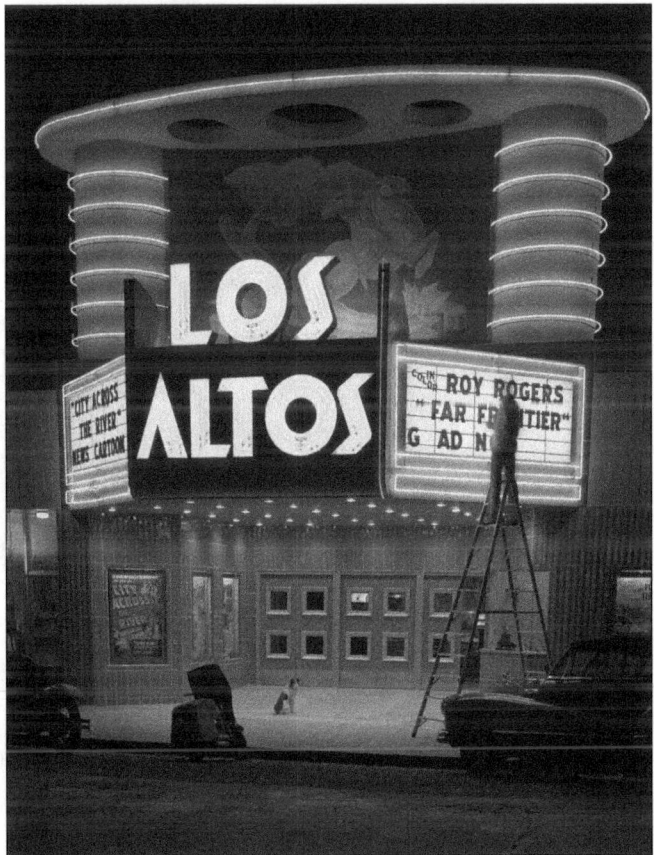

In its nighttime neon grandeur, Los Altos maintained its daytime illusion, only more so. A mural of a horse and rider above the marquee hinted at similar scenes on the auditorium walls done in shades of blue and green. Renamed Altos International in 1967, its final film offering was, appropriately enough, a free presentation of *The Last Picture Show* on January 19, 1977. It has since been redeveloped into offices and stores. (Los Altos History Museum.)

Judging from this 1910 photograph, there is no question that Mountain View's second moving picture theater, the Glen, located at 174 Castro Street (replacing an earlier one of the same name), was a family operation. Frederick L. "Fritz" Campen Jr. operated the theater, and his daughter Anna Campen played the piano. In 1921, a small Wurlitzer organ was installed. But the Campens had their eyes on building an even better showplace for their town. (History Center, Mountain View Public Library.)

Mountain View's Cinema Theatre, located at 892 Dana and Bryant Streets, was opened in 1934 by Antonio Blanco. In its later years, Spanish-language films, most of them imported from Mexico, were its primary attraction, but Noche de Banco (Bank Night) served its traditional purpose on Monday nights when audiences were more difficult to nail down. In this 1950 photograph, the jackpot is $105. The Cinema closed in the early 1950s and was torn down in 1955. (History Center, Mountain View Public Library.)

The Campen Theatre, designed by local architect Alexander Aimwell Cantin and located at 230 Castro Street in Mountain View, opened in 1926. It was named after its owner, Fritz Campen Jr. Later, Antonio Blanco added it to his local chain. By 1950, it maintained its updated 1930s appearance when it was renamed the Mountain View, and like its little sister the Cinema Theatre, it still used Bank Night to lure patrons on Wednesday evenings. A billboard over the box office flaunts a $350 jackpot. (History Center, Mountain View Public Library.)

In 1961, the Mountain View received a major overhaul and stylish new exterior. It closed in 1987 after a brief run as a Chinese cinema and was converted to showcase rock bands. Neil Young appeared there, as did heavy rockers Y&T. In 1995, the neon letters were pulled off, the decaying interior was remodeled, and a succession of nightclubs held sway for the next decade. Today, it is a restaurant and bar. (History Center, Mountain View Public Library.)

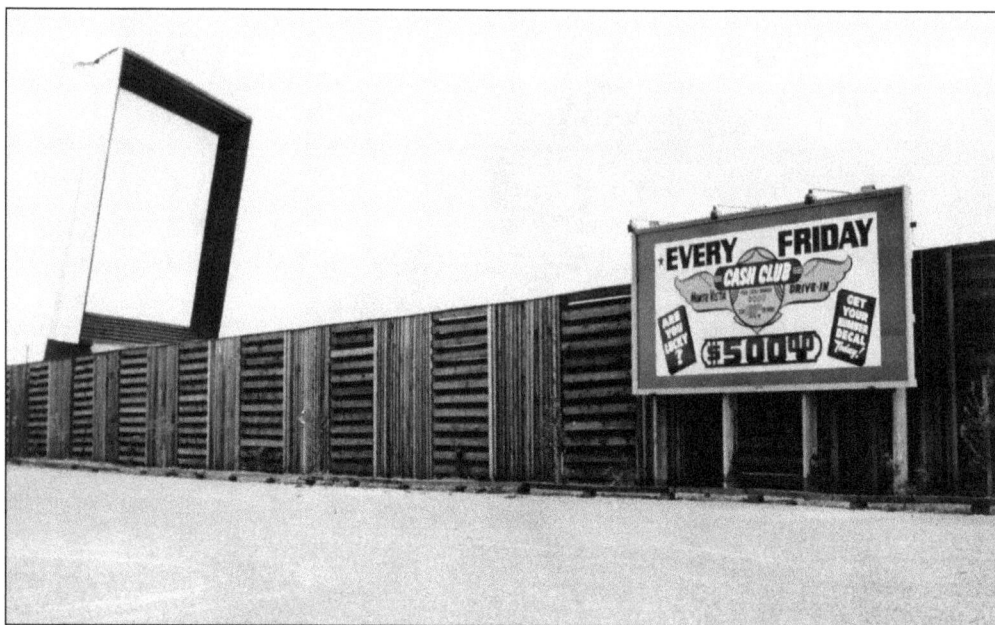

The Monte Vista Drive-In on Grant Road at El Camino Real in Mountain View opened on August 4, 1950. Taking a cue from its indoor rivals and doing them one better, Friday evening was Cash Club, with no less than a $500 jackpot. The happy winner was determined by a decal with the lucky number attached to his or her windshield. (History Center, Mountain View Public Library.)

Cars line up for Circus Days, another typical midweek drive-in promotion, heralding the beginning of the 1951 summer season. Showmanship was the order of the day, and audience response reflected the imagination of the entrepreneurs, which knew no bounds. About all patrons can expect today is, "Visit our website, something-or-other.com"—the less said, the better. Monte Vista closed in 1978 and was replaced by housing. (History Center, Mountain View Public Library.)

Located at 1500 North Shoreline Boulevard, the Moffett Drive-In, another Syufy enterprise, opened in 1964. Like its many brethren, Moffett later added screens, and by the time it closed in 1985 it had become a four-plex. The high visibility of its marquee from the Bayshore Freeway was a definite asset. (CinemaTour.)

As in the case of its sister theater, the Redwood Drive-In in Redwood City (pages 81–85), its acreage was too valuable to waste on a declining operation. Almost overnight, the Moffett disappeared, and the Century complex (pages 118–119) rose in its place.

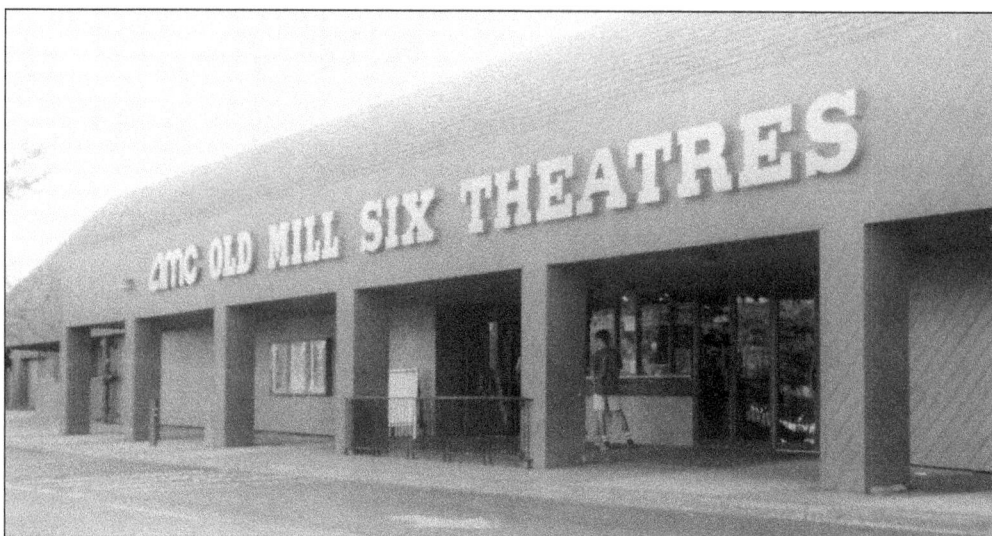

The Old Mill Six was another American Multi-Cinema (AMC) cookie-cutter shoebox multiplex design that operated from 1975 to 1994. It was located in a shopping center near the southwest corner of San Antonio Road and Showers Drive. The shopping center was intended to bring new life to the neighborhood. Even city officials openly admitted that the development never came close to meeting expectations, and the complex was eventually demolished, replaced by high-density housing.

Syufy Enterprises closed and demolished the main screen of the Moffett Drive-In in 1985 and began construction of its new Century 10 on the site. Once the new complex was far enough along, the remaining drive-in screens were closed, demolished, and converted to parking. Here, Dave Adams of Mountain View does carpentry work on the auditorium support beams, while one of the screens of the Moffett Drive-In looms in the background. (History Center, Mountain View Public Library.)

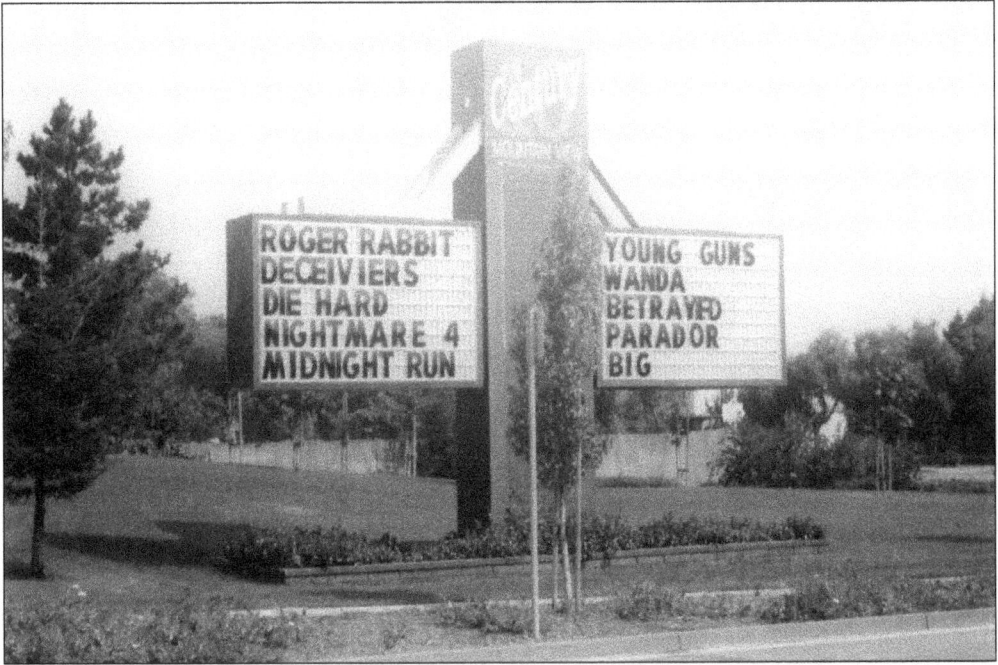

The Century 10 opened on November 1, 1985, at 1500 North Shoreline Boulevard on the land formerly occupied by the Moffett Drive-In. On July 22, 1994, it added six more screens and became Century Cinemas 16. Once again, Vincent Raney was Syufy's architect of choice to design yet another link in the expanding Century chain. Instead of his trademark domes, Raney had switched to polygonal auditoriums, though the additional six screens were rectangular.

Even in the age of cinematic architectural simplicity, Vincent Raney believed in adding a little innovation to his Modernist palette, including a traffic roundabout with a large fountain at its center. Once inside, patrons found themselves in a large lobby with plenty of room to relax and eat treats—even meals—from the concession counter before or after a show. A separate arcade room was provided for video-game enthusiasts. The Century 16 still thrives today.

With 6,500 reserved seats and 15,500 unreserved lawn locations, Shoreline Amphitheatre boasts a total seating capacity of 22,000. It was built in 1985–1986 by the City of Mountain View in cooperation with Bill Graham as part of the Shoreline Park Project. Today, it remains, without question, the peninsula's primary venue for live top-name pop and rock music presentations.

The New Strand in Sunnyvale opened around 1926 at 146–148 South Murphy Avenue next to the structure housing the old Strand, a nickelodeon. It was equipped with an organ and small stage. After it was renamed the Sunnyvale in 1935, Blanco's Peninsular Theaters took over the operation. The theater seated 934 in a stadium-style arrangement. A pair of arched windows presented a view over the marquee. The neon vertical sign was tall enough to be seen from El Camino Real. (AMPAS.)

Readers will find no better example of the abysmal austerity of 1960s architecture than this sad example of what happened to the hapless Sunnyvale. All original ornamentation had been stripped off, and the windows were plastered over. At the time of this 1980 photograph, intrepid moviegoers are offered two forgotten titles of the era, *Defiance* and *Star Virgin*, the details of which can be found on the Internet Movie Database (www.imdb.com).

121

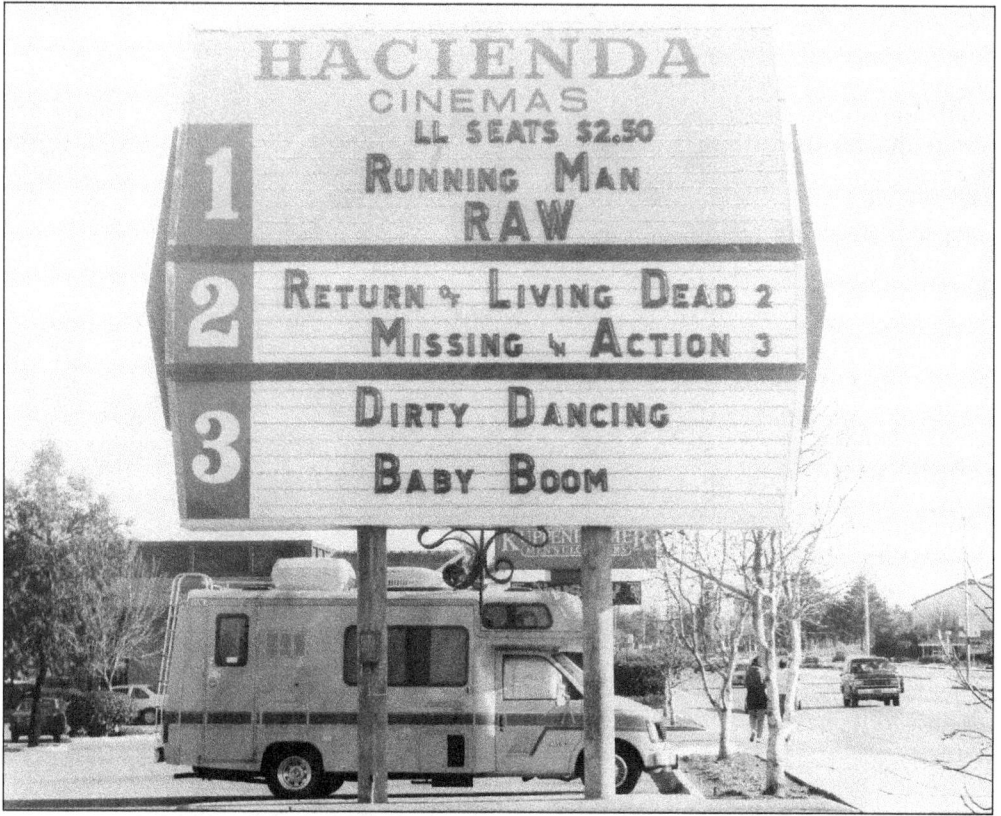

HACIENDA
CINEMAS
ALL SEATS $2.50
RUNNING MAN
RAW

RETURN 4 LIVING DEAD 2
MISSING 4 ACTION 3

DIRTY DANCING
BABY BOOM

An aptly named twin theater, Le Duet Cinema, opened at 738 El Camino Real in Sunnyvale in 1966. Ralph Shrader and his wife, Mimi, lived several blocks away on Kennard Way and were first in line at the opening; they were admitted free. The theater was set back from El Camino Real by a parking lot and beckoned to patrons with a pleasing neon sign in aqua-colored script. When one auditorium was divided, making the theater a tri-plex, a new name had to be found, so the theater took its name from its location in the Hacienda Shopping Center. The signage was somewhat hastily retrofitted to advertise the additional screen. This 1987 photograph (above), at which time the theater had adopted a double-feature bargain policy, demonstrates that titles can make for odd—even embarrassing—combinations. In the case of all three screens' offerings, the imagination can conjure up things that were not intended, but at least the pairing of *Dirty Dancing* and *Baby Boom* possesses a certain sequential logic. In the 1990s, the entire shopping center was rebuilt from the ground up, leaving only the name Hacienda to hint at what once was.

On a piece of land bounded by Lawrence Expressway, Reed Avenue, and Aster Avenue, Syufy Enterprises built a typical 1960s drive-in. The Sunnyvale was entered via Aster Avenue. Not only was the Sunnyvale Drive-In's architecture typical but also was the fare presented on-screen. *The Venetian Affair* and *Glass Bottom Boat*, the latter a 1966 release starring Doris Day, seem harmless enough, but screen two's *Queen of Blood* and *Blood Bath* were hardly chamber of commerce–worthy material. Today, the site is occupied by condominiums and a small shopping center. More can be learned about theaters in Sunnyvale and the rest of the South Bay in *Theatres of San Jose* (Arcadia, 2009). (CinemaTour.)

The two-screen Serra opened on Calaveras Boulevard in the Serra Center in Milpitas. Typical of cinemas built in the late 1960s and early 1970s, it was a plain but substantial structure; the streamlined shopping center designs of the postwar years were abandoned in favor of a more rustic approach. It became an outlet for double features at bargain prices and now shows films from India. (Gary Lee Parks.)

The tentacles of AMC found their way to Milpitas, and another cookie-cutter example of shoebox cinema emerged as the imaginatively named AMC 10, located at 577 East Calaveras Boulevard. One innovation was the introduction of armrest cup holders, now taken for granted in cinemas everywhere. It has since been superseded by the Great Mall 20 (next page).

The Great Mall in Milpitas, which is exactly what its name implies, was built from a former automobile manufacturing plant. At the north end stands Century Theatres' Great Mall 20. It blends hints of the past, such as a sweeping entrance canopy and the use of neon, with those of the future—LED reader boards announce the attractions—in an age where technology strives to find new ways to get people to come out of their houses for respite from their hectic lives. (Gary Lee Parks.)

INDEX

Visit us at
arcadiapublishing.com

www.ingramcontent.com/pod-product-compliance
Lightning Source LLC
Chambersburg PA
CBHW050602110426
42813CB00008B/2433